WOMEN AND WARRIORS
OF THE PLAINS

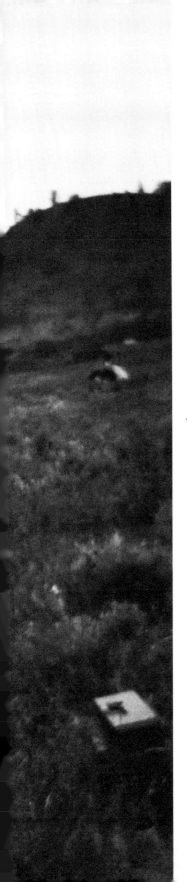

WOMEN AND WARRIORS OF THE PLAINS

The Pioneer Photography of
Julia E. Tuell

Dan Aadland

9 Dec '97
To Susan, recalling
our meeting at the Western Heritage
Center and with appreciation for your
interest,
Dan Aadland

MACMILLAN • USA

ALSO BY DAN AADLAND
Horseback Adventures

MACMILLAN
A Simon & Schuster Macmillan Company
1633 Broadway
New York, NY 10019

Library of Congress Cataloging-in-Publication Data
Aadland, Dan.
    Women and Warriors of the Plains: the pioneer
    photography of Julia E. Tuell/Dan Aadland.
        p. cm.
    Includes bibliographical references.
    ISBN 0-87605-748-2
        1. Cheyenne Indians—Portraits.   2. Cheyenne Indians—
Social life and customs—Pictorial works.   3. Tuell, Julia E.   I. Title.
E99. C53A23   1996   96-9380
978' 004973—dc20   CIP
10 9 8 7 6 5 4 3 2 1

Printed in the United States of America

BOOK DESIGN BY GEORGE J. McKEON

Title page: Julia E. Tuell at her camera photographing a Northern Cheyenne Sun Dance near Lame Deer, Montana, 1909.

Varble Tuell, October 1995.

*To Varble Tuell, Julia's youngest child, my friend,
without whom this book would never have come to be:
an artist, a gentleman, and the one who steadfastly
realized the power of his mother's work. This is his
book and Julia's, not mine.*

*"I want," he said, "a book that will be a tribute to
my mother. She was a pioneer woman, and I am proud
to be her son."*

CONTENTS

FOREWORD: BY FATHER PETER J. POWELL XI

ACKNOWLEDGMENTS XV

A NOTE ON TERMINOLOGY XVII

INVOCATION XIX

JULIA 1

THE WOMEN 41

DAILY LIFE 74

THE WARRIORS 103

THE OTHER LIFE 137

POSTLUDE 173

NOTES 177

SOME INTERESTING BOOKS 181

FOREWORD

A SPECIAL REVERENCE FILLED THE VOICE of Henry Little Coyote, Keeper of Esevone, whenever he spoke of the Massaum, the sacred ceremony in which the animals dance. Born in 1875, during the final days of Cheyenne freedom, he was the son of White Frog, chief priest of the Massaum on seven different occasions. Thus Little Coyote knew well the sanctity of the Massaum. In 1959, at eighty-four winters of age, he was chosen Keeper of Esevone, one of the Two Great Covenants of the Cheyenne People, and the greatest spiritual treasure of the Northern Cheyenne tribe. During the years in which I was privileged to be instructed by him, he and Weasel Woman, his wife, lived in or by the Sacred Hat tipi. But even in the indescribably holy presence of Esevone herself, Little Coyote's voice radiated a unique reverence whenever he spoke of the Massaum.

The same was true of the other elders who shared memories of the Massaum with me: Frank Waters, Willis Medicine Bull, John Fire Wolf, Josephine Head Swift Limpy, Joe Tall Bull and Charles White Dirt among them. The holiness of what they saw never left them, filling their voices with wonder as they described the supernatural power displayed by the animals as they danced. And among them were persons to whom the yellow wolf, holiest of the animals in the Massaum, continued to make his presence known, his voice rising out of the darkness of night: powerful, mysterious, unmistakable.

The Massaum or Animal Dance of August 1911 is the heart of Julia Tuell's remarkable photographic legacy. With the exception of Edward S. Curtis's portraits of the Southern Cheyenne Massaum of 1927, nearly a generation later, few photographs exist of this exceedingly sacred but little-known ceremony. Important too is the fact that Julia Tuell's pictures preserve portraits of the oldest holy men and holy women among the Northern Cheyennes in the early 1900s, priests and priestesses who knew and offered the Massaum in its most ancient existing form. These included priests such as Iron Shirt, born ca. 1831; White Frog, born ca. 1842 and in 1911 a Council Chief as well; and Tall White Man, born ca. 1847. Island Woman, the chief Instructor woman, was born ca. 1847, and the members of the Young Wolves society who participated in the 1911 Massaum were venerable women as well.

The 1911 Massaum was unique in that for the first time white persons were allowed to witness and record holy rites. Today, as in the past, traditionalist Cheyenne priests admonish all persons participating in offering the sacred ceremonies to be in harmony with one another, to respect each other, for only then will all the Cheyenne People and all creation be fully blessed. That harmony was displayed in the 1911 Massaum, where the Cheyenne participants and the two white observers, Julia Tuell and George Bird Grinnell, worked together in mutual respect in offering and recording the sacred rites.

George Bird Grinnell, the white scholar who knew the Cheyenne best, had known them since 1874. In 1890 he began interviewing the elders, returning each year to record their history and culture with a respect and accuracy that remains unrivaled. The Cheyenne People trusted "Bird," as they named Grinnell. Thus when he requested permission to record the Massaum, the chiefs, headmen and priests, gathered in council, granted him permission to do so. However, trusted as Grinnell was, he was still a stranger, a non-Cheyenne. Thus at the beginning of the Massaum, White Frog, the chief priest, offered a prayer to the Ma'heono, the Sacred Powers, asking them to pardon him for revealing these things to an enemy, that is, a stranger—Grinnell himself. And although Grinnell was permitted to see and record the public ceremonies, he was not permitted to witness those holy rites in which the Sacred Woman, the Pledger's wife, made her offering. (Grinnell was, however, aware that this offering was both made and hidden from him.)

Julia Tuell's most important photographs were taken on the holiest day of the Massaum—the fifth day—when sacred power flowed at its greatest intensity. Her camera was focused on the Massaum lodge, where the holiest rites were offered, the holiest work done. Thus she succeeded in capturing the two most sacred events of the public ceremonies: the yellow wolf's entrance into the world outside the Massaum lodge; and the yellow wolf's hide exposed for veneration, blessing the people who came and prayed before him. And she made photographs of the other participants as well, as can be seen in these pages.

The key person in Julia Tuell's being granted permission to photograph the Massaum is surely American Horse, the chief she admired and who, in turn, felt a special friendship for her and her family. Seventy-seven winters old, he had been chief of the So'taaeo'o band since 1874. By 1911, however, he was one of the Four Old Man Chiefs, the priest-chiefs who were head chiefs of the Northern Cheyenne People. American Horse's priestly power was that of the Massaum lodge, and it was considerable, for he had long been the yellow wolf, that animal possessing the greatest sacred power in the ceremony. Recently, however, he had passed the wearing of the yellow wolf hide to Spotted Elk, a younger man, who was yellow wolf in the ceremonies Julia Tuell was photographing now. American Horse, however, retained his power as both Massaum priest and Old Man Chief, power which surely influenced the other chiefs, priests and headmen in granting Julia Tuell permission to photograph the holy ceremonies unfolding before her camera now.

That which she preserved appears in the following pages and also in *The Cheyenne Indians* by George Bird Grinnell, the most important published work devoted to the Cheyenne People. Grinnell's recording of the 1911 Massaum appears in Volume II. Sensitive, accurate, respectful, it reflects his profound respect for the Cheyenne and their sacred ceremonies. But words alone fail to capture the power of the Animal Dance. Julia Tuell's photographs come to our assistance here. For in them we glimpse such mysteries as the yellow wolf coming forth from the Massaum lodge, radiating power, and the reverence manifested by the people as they prayed before the yellow wolf hide, confident they would receive the blessings they requested. And in the faces of the priests, holy women and participants we see reflected the strength of the Cheyenne People, a holy people.

Thus Julia Tuell's greatest legacy remains her capturing and preserving of the mystery and power of the last great Massaum among the Northern Cheyenne People, that final offering of the holy ceremony where the animals dance, bringing blessing, healing and renewed life to the Cheyenne People and their world.

Father Peter John Powell
author of *Sweet Medicine*
and *People of the Sacred Mountain*

Acknowledgments

In addition to Varble Tuell, Julia's son, without whose dogged determination and herculean effort this book could not have been written, I would like to thank Father Peter J. Powell for his wonderful assistance in reading the manuscript, offering clarification and writing the foreword. Ruby Sooktis of Lame Deer and Paul Dyke, the artist and scholar of the Buffalo People, lent their counsel. My wife, Emily, who believed so strongly in the project from its first beginnings, furnished motivation when my own faith flagged, then served as personal editor and organizer.

A Note on Terminology

It is appropriate that we are sensitive to the names we use for ethnic and religious groups. It is perhaps less appropriate that we occasionally single out just one term as acceptable and "politically correct," the implication then being that all others are disrespectful.

The term most currently in vogue for the indigenous peoples of North America is Native American, with which I have no quarrel, although I note a linguistic inaccuracy: "Native" means to have been born in the location named (to which all Americans but immigrants can lay claim). I like rather better a term used in the publicity materials of a Sioux folk singer, "Original Americans." Perhaps that one will catch on.

Meanwhile I continue to see letters to the editor of the *The Billings Gazette* here in Montana from Crow and Cheyenne people who prefer the term "Indian," a tribal designation or most distinctly "Indian People" or "Cheyenne People," which if heard orally place a unique accent on the first syllable of "people."

Similar questions arise with English renditions of Native American words. Both "Sioux" and "Crow" are English translations of names given those tribes by their enemies and are certainly not as accurate or respectful as those with which the tribes termed themselves (Lakota and Absaroka, respectively). But English words of more than a century longevity communicate well, so I have not completely abandoned them. The reader will also note variations in spellings of Cheyenne and Sioux words, the reason being that orthography—the representation of non-English words to approximate the correct pronunciation—improves with time and further study.

I make these notes only to remind the reader that it is the feelings lying behind any of these designations with which we should concern ourselves. Levels of acceptability coupled with any particular terminology have changed, and will change, with the times. But feelings of utmost respect for the cultures and people pictured and discussed in this book are the very reason Julia Tuell took the photos, and are a primary motivation for my writing this book.

INVOCATION

FOR ONE WHO HAS ENJOYED the privilege of knowing the work of Julia Tuell, words such as "favorite" seem pale and inappropriate. The collection is so rich and powerful that dozens of the photographs beg to be singled out. But the one on the facing page synthesizes for me what Julia Tuell and her camera were all about. True, this is simply a snapshot without the artistic composition or poignancy of theme evident in much of the collection. It was not even snapped by Julia herself. But this casual grouping of Julia Tuell with her daughters Wenonah and Julia Mae and her baby Carl, held by the great Cheyenne chief American Horse, speaks volumes on the relationship of a remarkable woman to the Native American people who were her friends for much of her adult life.

Look at the postures of the little girls who squint against the sun. They may know that the man behind them was among the Cheyennes who fought against George Armstrong Custer on that terrible Sunday in 1876, but if they do it is of little consequence to them; they know American Horse as the grandfatherly man who stops in to have coffee with their parents often, and their casual stances show that. Julia's posture is also casual, although one wonders by the look on her face if she is concerned that her husband will properly manipulate the camera standing on its tripod. American Horse himself stands more rigidly. He is now, in 1909, a veteran of dozens of portrait sessions, formal in nature. And yet one senses that this is not the only time he has held the baby.

So I offer this photograph as an invocation to the book. In an age that too often stresses divisions between the races and sexes we need occasional reminders of the humanity that links us all, of the human understanding that transcends such differences, an understanding that can make great beauty in even the most tragic of times. It was this understanding between Julia Tuell and her subjects that made these photographs possible.

Left to right, Wenonah, 7; American Horse holding the baby Carl; Julia Mae, 4; and Julia Tuell.

WOMEN AND WARRIORS OF THE PLAINS

JULIA

AT THE BEGINNING OF THIS CENTURY a petite teenage girl named Julia Toops met a visitor at her parents' home in Louisville, Kentucky. The man, a school teacher for more than twenty years in southern Indiana and Kentucky, was twenty-seven years older than she. Such an age difference would be highly unusual today, but perhaps was less so in a time when older, steady, established gentlemen were considered desirable matches. We have no chain of correspondence between the two to reveal what drew Julia to this serious-looking professional man, but one might guess at part of the attraction: The man had plans, exciting ones. No, he was not returning to a quiet rural school in Indiana. He had joined government service and was off to the far reaches of northern Minnesota to teach Indians, Chippewa Indians, and if he was adventuresome enough at forty-one to tackle such a career change, his eyes must have sparkled when he talked about it.

Everything I know about Julia E. Tuell from twenty years of studying her photographs and an equal time saturated with the stories told by her son, my friend Varble, everything I can glean, suggests to me that a yearning for adventure must have been tied to the other emotions that led Julia to marry P.V. Tuell on April 13, 1901. True, it was not a conventional thing to do. But we can be thankful that Julia, like great men and women everywhere, was not content to stay conventional. At the time she was married the battle of the Little Bighorn was just twenty-five years past. The terrible events at Wounded Knee had occurred only a decade earlier. She would live to know some of the participants in both events, to photograph them, to serve them coffee and to learn their language. She would sense, better than many frontier photographers, the importance of the look in a school child's eye. She would understand the need to preserve culture, whether exotic dances and ceremonies or mundane tasks of living and surviving. She would grow to be loved and trusted by the members of several tribes, and this in the early reservation years, an era absolutely gutwrenching for Native Americans. This trust in Julia would open doors, would allow the shutter of her Eastman Kodak camera to click on scenes normally barred to whites.

Julia with her father, William Toops, her mother, Elizabeth, and her sister, Violet, at their home in Louisville, Kentucky, 1903. Julia is holding her first baby, Wenonah.

But all that had to wait a few years. The sixteen-year-old bride first went to an island in Vermilion Lake, Minnesota (on the Chippewa Indian reservation with the same name), for her first few years as a schoolmaster's wife. Varble can remember stories of Chippewa hunters drifting along the shore in birchbark canoes, looking for moose. Hunting at night with lanterns, the Chippewa men would float up to a moose, which was preoccupied by the light long enough to provide a shot with bow and arrow. The winters were intensely cold, and during the first one, on a February morning fifty-below, Julia gave birth to a baby,

One of the few Tuell photographs from the Sisseton Sioux Reservation in eastern South Dakota, 1905. Wenonah stands beside a Sioux woman holding Julia Mae (at seven weeks).

Wenonah. That winter the ice froze on the lake six feet thick. When the couple crossed the lake that spring there was still jagged ice, and Julia feared it would scrape a hole in the bottom of the boat.

Through this experience and their next on the Sisseton Sioux reservation in eastern South Dakota, Julia apparently had no camera of quality, for her first photos of note date from their third reservation, the Northern Cheyenne in Montana, where they moved in 1906. But perhaps experiences with the Chippewa and the Sisseton Sioux served to alert Julia to the great human drama that passed before her eyes like a fleeting western autumn, soon to be gone.

In any case, at Lame Deer, Montana, on the reservation of the Northern Cheyennes, Julia became a photographer, a great one, her stature as such having largely escaped until now the attention it deserves. This was not a time in history when a woman could select photography as a paying career, eschewing family and other considerations. There was, by this time, a second daughter, Julia Mae, and a host of things to be done to maintain a proper household in these days before push-button conveniences. But her photographs exude enthusiasm, and her attention to detail shows the eye of an artist. When she filmed the site of the Custer battle she insisted on doing so on the same day of the year (June 25) as the battle actually occurred, so that the prairie grasses and sagebrush would be at a similar stage. But perhaps more important even than her attention to detail, Julia's photographs show a grasp of what is important.

And this grasp cannot be underemphasized in any artistic endeavor. I once heard a professor of writing give a graduate student a scathing review of his short story. The characterization was poor, the action moved haltingly and there were grammatical difficulties. The poor student finally asked whether he should give up writing and pursue another line of interest. "Oh no," the professor told him. "You have something going for you that more than makes up for these difficulties. You have a sense of the important, a feel for what is worth writing about in the first place. Just keep working." Julia E. Tuell had this sense of the important. Every click of the shutter meant expense and time plus painstaking effort to produce a quality print. She directed her camera at the things she considered worth photographing, and her taste was impeccable. Yes, she gave us more of the wonderful portraits of Indian chiefs in full regalia that we have come to expect from photographers of the era. But she also gave us details of reservation life, from jerking meat to pounding chokecherries to butchering dogs for meat. There are little girls playing with dolls around miniature tepees and little boys with bows and arrows, ready to be warriors. There are political rallies for troops returning from Europe during World War I with placards that say "Damn the Kaiser," and there are Indian ceremonies of the most serious sort, the Sun

Julia and P.V. Tuell in Cheyenne clothing, 1906.

Dance and the Massaum, in those years rapidly disappearing from the face of the prairie and usually barred to white photographers.

The early years on the Northern Cheyenne reservation in southeast Montana seem to have been happy ones for Julia and her husband and babies, if their demeanor in the photos is an indication. This was their first experience in the Rocky Mountain West. Under its huge skies they must have smelled the sage and heard the meadowlark (three descending notes, then up to a triumphant trill). South, nearby, were the Bighorn Mountains, then southwest, the Pryors, and finally, a blue line when viewed from the hilltops around Lame Deer, the Absarokas. There was much to do for a young, energetic mother, plenty of space to play for her growing family. Perhaps Julia (like my own mother, also a young prairie wife) found a different butte to climb every Sunday afternoon.

Not all was idyllic, however. The Tuells customarily returned to Kentucky during summer vacation. In the spring of 1908 they took a wagon to Crow Agency to catch their train east. (The Crow reservation in Montana borders the Northern Cheyenne, and the nearest railhead was at the settlement called Crow Agency.) Once on the train, Julia, late in another pregnancy, began to feel ill, and the family requested a stop in Gillette, Wyoming, to seek a doctor. Julia lost the baby, a boy. No coffin so small was available, so P.V. Tuell, an active Mason, looked up the Masonic group in Gillette. Its members built a tiny cedar coffin, and Julia buried her baby there. It is living that makes us understand the living of others, sorrow that makes us understand sorrow. The race or color of other human beings becomes irrelevant when we live their sorrows and joys along with them. So it is no mystery that

Julia and Julia Mae before the framework of a Cheyenne sweat lodge, 1907.

Woostah (Vo'estaa'e) and Wenonah.

Julia's photographs depict Indian mothers who mourn their lost children, who put them in wooden boxes and cover them with rocks. Nearly fifty years later, in 1956, Varble took Julia back to Gillette to find the grave of her lost boy. At the courthouse, by sheer coincidence, an old caretaker overheard her request for directions to the grave and took Varble and Julia there. She ordered a stone for the grave.

A little more than a year after losing her baby in Gillette, Julia gave birth to Carl. (Indeed, she was pregnant with Carl—just two weeks from delivery—when she stood behind her tripod in the photograph that is on the title page of this book.) She was learning the Cheyenne language now, helped by the wisdom of a frequent visitor, Chief American Horse. (She would also meet and photograph the well-known Sioux chief of the same name.) She understood that American Horse knew no English, so she communicated as best she could without words, then began learning Cheyenne, finally becoming able to converse with him. Two years later he said to her a sentence in broken but perfectly understandable English. "American Horse," she said, "I thought you knew no English." He told her, simply, that if he had spoken English to her she would have had no incentive to learn Cheyenne. He had trained her as he wished.

Life during these years at Lame Deer was always interesting, sometimes lively. There was the day Wenonah was missing. All parents can envision it: worries compounding, thoughts of a small child drowned in the creek or being kidnapped, panic that cuts through the heart. Finally, when all the worst had been fantasized, an old Cheyenne lady appeared, White Cow, "Woostah," (Vo'estaa'e) walking casually toward the house, the baby on her back.[1] They had been to the store for candy. Little Wenonah had been furnished day care by White Cow, the daughter of the great chief Morning Star (Dull Knife).

And through these years, becoming a constant companion, a recorder of visions, was the camera, an Eastman Kodak 8 ×10 glass-plate camera. Kodak had introduced large-format roll film two decades earlier, so Julia's camera was not a modern one, even for its time. She probably purchased it mail order directly from the Eastman Kodak Company. Always, of course, she used a tripod, for the camera was heavy and shutter speeds were slow.

Afterwards, she developed the negatives in her makeshift darkroom. Varble remembers the contact-printing process quite well. He still has the wooden frame that held the glass-plate negative securely against the printing paper. Holding the frame facing the kerosene lamp, his mother allowed light to shine on the plate for four minutes, timing it with a wind-up alarm clock. Then she doused the print for the required time in porcelain trays of the proper chemicals. The prints she wished to glaze were put face down on a special metal plate. Varble recalls her rolling the prints onto the shiny black surface of this large (approximately four feet square) piece of steel. When dry, the prints would loosen and emerge with a glossy finish. And, in these days before color film, when black and white did not satisfy her, Julia learned to hand-tint her photographs with watercolors.

Photography, like writing and painting, is a type of communication. The photographer's art consists of letting light into a camera for a very brief moment in time. The photographer chooses the time and place and path of light, and thus chooses the image that touches the film. If all goes perfectly, the image preserved is exactly what the photographer sought.

As we have said, Julia had an eye for that worth preserving, and she also had the good fortune to be exposed to moments in time that begged to be frozen. Lame Deer, from 1906 to 1912, presented perhaps the last opportunity to pictorially preserve the Northern Cheyenne tribe in a state not too distant from its free-roaming past. When Julia and her husband arrived at Lame Deer, all Cheyennes older than thirty had lived during the era preceding the Custer fight. Many who fought against Crook at the Rosebud and Custer at the Little Bighorn were only in middle age, and the stigma against talking about those events, the fear that admitting involvement could bring retaliation, had largely faded.

The adult Cheyennes still intimately knew all the skills needed for day-to-day survival on the prairie. Making jerky, pitching lodges, sewing skin clothing, crafting and using bows and arrows—all these were still immediate realities.

Rigging a travois to carry cargo behind dog or horse was a universal skill still fresh in the minds of these formerly mobile people. To know the members of this tribe at this point in history was a great privilege, and Julia Tuell's photographs show her appreciation.

As Julia knew them in the early twentieth century, the Northern Cheyenne were a people who had just survived a traumatic generation. Their saga from the early nineteenth century until the reservation days is the stuff of epic poems. Only a century or so before Julia Tuell met the Cheyenne People at Lame Deer, the tribe was emerging from a more eastern, agricultural existence. Before the late 1700s, the Cheyennes most likely occupied the lake country of the northern Mississippi drainage. A hundred years later, according to Father Peter J. Powell in *Sweet Medicine*, there were still elderly Cheyennes who could recall stories and songs of a day before the buffalo and the horse, before, even, the Sun Dance, an age when the tribe planted corn and squash in the fertile soil of the bottomlands along the rivers in the upper Midwest.[2]

Drastic changes took place late in the eighteenth century, however. The Cheyennes acquired the horse, the ultimate machine for converting bison on the hoof to jerky on the meat pole, and they also had serious conflict with neighbors, both Indian and white. Some tribes, such as the Chippewa, were already trading partners with white civilization and had acquired firearms from Hudson's Bay Company, a decided edge.

Thus, by the early nineteenth century, the Cheyennes had become people of the northern Great Plains, people of the horse and the buffalo hunt, people who waged war with some neighboring tribes and allied themselves with others. For perhaps only a century or so, in that slot of time between their emerging onto the Plains and their eventual domination by encroaching white civilization, the Cheyennes enjoyed an existence that has been the romantic envy of much of the world. Though not without hardship and danger, the nomadic life of these people epitomizes to many a life of freedom. Not tied to a particular location, the Cheyennes went where the grass was good and where game was to be found. Their high-protein diet seems to have promoted health and generous stature.

Gradually the tribe drifted westward, eventually coming to consider Bear Butte, a prominent terrain feature midway between the present-day towns of Sturgis and Belle Fourche, South Dakota, to be the spiritual center of their home. (Years later, in the winter of 1929–1930, Varble Tuell hunted and gathered wood within sight of Bear Butte in the nearby Black Hills.) Native Americans did not think in terms of absolute boundaries, of course. Borders, deeds and survey lines were alien ideas until introduced by white men, usually when treaties were being drawn. But a certain region was considered a homeland. Not felt to be owned exclusively, the home country was thought of as the place one belonged and was happy. By the mid-nineteenth century, what is now western South Dakota and Nebraska and the eastern fringes of Wyoming and Montana had become the domain of the Northern Cheyenne and several of the bands of the Teton Lakota (Sioux).

There is no need here to recount the chaotic events between the signing of the 1868 Laramie Treaty and the final submission of the Sioux to the white reservation system, symbolized by the terrible events at Wounded Knee during the winter of 1890–1891. It is adequate to say that the Cheyennes, though a much smaller tribe than the Sioux, were major players. Among the most independent of all tribes, the Cheyennes allied themselves with those bands of Sioux most determined to continue their old way of life, most defiant of U.S. government authority, most resentful of promises and treaties broken. Like the Cheyennes, the Sioux had pushed gradually westward, had come to occupy land once thought of as Crow and Shoshoni country. Those two tribes considered the Sioux and Cheyenne, more than the white man, the invaders of their territory, and thus allied themselves with the U.S. Army. Indeed, the battle of the Little Bighorn was fought on land that was, even in 1876, part of the Crow Reservation. In Cheyenne eyes the reservation borders were meaningless; they believed the Little Bighorn country to be on their ancestral land.

That terrible battle and the stopping of General George A. Crook a week earlier on the Rosebud were great victories for the Sioux and Cheyenne, but they were also exceedingly temporary ones. Among the American population there had been a strong movement, more powerful than Americans today seem to realize, sympathetic to the plight of Native Americans. For many with such leanings, the wiping out of Custer and his contingent of the Seventh Cavalry had much the same effect that Pearl Harbor was to have later on those Americans reluctant to enter World War II. Thus Sunday, June 25, 1876, was not the sort of turning point one normally associates with great victories. The Sioux mystic Black Elk, then a boy of fourteen, said the massive alliance of Sioux and Cheyenne stopped fighting because "they were sick of the smell of blood." They could have turned their efforts against Major Marcus A. Reno, Captain Frederick W. Benteen and the others, dug in on a hilltop four miles southeast of the ridge where Custer died and, no doubt, have wiped them out too, making the military success even more spectacular. Instead, the various tribal bands packed up their gear and dispersed.

What followed was a year where the military, led by savvy, experienced generals such as Crook, got the authorization it needed to pursue the remaining hostile Indians and return them to the agencies. The pressure was relentless. Harassed, chased and starved, one by one the bands came into the reservations and laid down their arms. By the summer of 1877, few remained at large.

Although the Northern Cheyenne had a brief respite at Camp Robinson in northwest Nebraska, they now faced another fight, this time a political one. This was the sort of battle for which their great prowess as warriors was little help. Much of what is now Oklahoma had been set aside as Indian Territory, a great reservation, and there was tremendous pressure to force the Northern Cheyenne to join their relatives, the Southern Cheyenne, in that sector. After all, they were told, the northern people had often traveled there to see their relatives in the past, and they would be welcomed. The Northern Cheyenne steadfastly refused to go, for the north was home. Their sacred mountain and their best memories were in the north country.

But pressure prevailed, and in May 1877, nearly a thousand Northern Cheyennes were escorted by the army to the reservation of their relatives to the south, from whom they had been separate for a generation. They were soon terribly unhappy. It was very hot in this southern country. Friction with the Southern Cheyenne, sickness that took many lives and longing for their home-land enveloped the Northern Cheyennes, and they pleaded to be sent north again. The Cheyenne historian John Stands In Timber told Father Peter J. Powell of a woman who typified the feelings of her people:

> An old Northern woman, dying of malaria, voiced this longing for the pine hills rising along the valleys of the Rosebud and the Tongue. In the midst of her fever she murmured, "Up north, the pines make a rustling sound in the wind, and the trees smell good." Then she fell back and died.[3]

When persuasion failed, a band of men, women and children under the leadership of Little Wolf fled Indian Territory for the country the Cheyennes considered home. A lost tribe searching for Israel, their tale is evocative of all human epics that involve a wandering people trying desperately to return to a land they love and call home. Chased, then attacked at every turn, this band avoided fighting when they could, not shooting until fired upon, but to little avail. Yet, a little less than a year after their exile began, what was left of Little Wolf's band did reach the valley of the Yellowstone.

Other bands of the Northern Cheyenne had parallel experiences, the imprisonment of Morning Star (Dull Knife) and his people and their eventual suicidal clash with an army carrying out the order to send them south being one of the most tragic of all. But while it's difficult to classify any relegation to reservation life as a happy ending for Plains Indians, the Northern Cheyenne struggle did eventually result in realization of a promise made to the people by General Nelson A. Miles. The Northern Cheyenne did get their reservation, did get it in the country not too far from their sacred mountain. When Miles showed Cheyenne leaders the land he intended to propose for their reservation they said it was just right—there was no use looking any further. And it was on this piece of land, for which so many Cheyennes shed blood, this reservation headquartered at Lame Deer, Montana, that Julia Tuell met them.

The photographs in this book show just how well she came to know the Northern Cheyenne people. P.V. Tuell, Julia's husband, was the schoolmaster in a system of reservation schools that is often considered controversial today. The school, after all, was the institution charged with "civilizing" Native Americans. This meant, in the eyes of many, making them as "white" as possible, and the term "going back to the blanket" was often used pejoratively during this era to mean going back to native ways.

But it's fair to point out that it was not only schools on Indian reservations during the late nineteenth and early twentieth centuries that were given the duty of making everyone "American." This was the age when "hyphenated" citizens were to be assimilated. No longer were you to be an Irish-American or an Italian-American, just an American (and one suspects the people of that day would be surprised to know that hyphenating is again popular today). Children of European immigrants were expected to shed their native customs and languages along with their coats when they entered the school.

A friend tells me of a Swedish family who immigrated to central Montana at the turn of the century. The daughter entered school knowing no English and simply received an "F" grade on everything she turned in. By the middle of the year the girl was able to intersperse some English words with her Swedish and began getting "C's." By the end of the year the girl (who must have been highly intelligent) was writing perfect English and "A's" now adorned her papers. My own father entered an inner-city school speaking only Norwegian. His playmates spoke primarily Italian. The teachers spoke only English, and Dad learned it, quickly, to survive. We flinch at such harshness today, perhaps while reluctantly admitting its effectiveness.

Appreciation for minority cultures and languages was generally rare during the early twentieth century in America. I was once tasked with writing the history of a German Lutheran church in Jordan, Montana. Discovering a gap of several years in the church records, I asked for an explanation and was directed to the town doctor, an elderly man who was supposed to "know everything." After chiding me, a teacher, for not knowing the answer, he reminded me of a

First day at the log cabin school at Lame Deer, 1907. This Cheyenne boy is sad, Julia said, because his braids must be cut before entering school.

federal law passed during World War I making it illegal to speak German in a public place. The German-American pastor and the ranchers who made up his congregation, American citizens all, knew no English, so worship had to be suspended until the ban was lifted.

We must consider the climate of the times and the things American culture expected of schools before we judge reservation schools too harshly. Then we admire Julia Tuell all the more. She captures the haunting sadness in the eyes of a Cheyenne boy about to enter school, understands his distress in knowing he must part with his braided hair. American schools believed in uniformity, so the hair of young Indian boys was cut. But hair was an extremely important part of Plains Indian culture. Commonly, a brave tended not only his own hair but fixed his wife's hair as well. Hair was considered to be part of their strength. Again, we must consider time and place and not-too-pleasant realities. Head lice were a terrible problem in schools of the day, and long hair was thought to encourage them.

None of this is intended to minimize the terrible impact caused by the unrealistic expectations of an advanced white civilization that thought a culture thousands of years old could simply put on different clothing, learn another language and adopt a way of life utterly foreign, and do this, neatly, within a decade or two. The Dawes Act, which was passed by Congress in 1887, reflected this belief. Well-intentioned enough, it broke the reservations into 160-acre allotments for each head of family, the idea being to put the Native American family on par with white homesteaders. It failed, of course, to recognize the depth and importance of culture.

At one point a set of shiny new farm equipment was delivered to the Northern Cheyennes. There was a plow, a disk, a harrow and a drill along with harnesses for the horses, truly an Iowa farmer's dream. The Cheyennes simply stared. Even horse-drawn farm equipment is quite technical, a product of generations of accumulated knowledge passed down from father to son. Apparently no one in an official capacity had suspected the Cheyennes would lack the faintest idea what to do with this equipment. More, a civilization based on European culture, which considered every tillable patch of ground precious, could not imagine a culture that considered turning sod upside down to be a foolish crime. Why, asked the Cheyennes, would you turn under the grass that gave life and strength to the buffalo and therefore the people? Why would you make the green ground look black?

A seldom-mentioned sadness in the Plains Indian experience was this: From their new reservation life the people could see their old, free life. One thinks of the ancient tale of a man imprisoned in the turret of a castle who could see, from

Skeletons of the past.

P.V. Tuell posing with buffalo skulls at Lame Deer, ca. 1907. The rifle is a prop for the photo. The skulls are from years earlier; many could be found lying on the prairie at this time.

a distance, the day-to-day life of the woman he loved. Yes, it was fine that the Crow and Cheyenne and many of the Sioux were granted reservations in vicinities they called home. But it must have been torturous, too, to look on prairies that now held no buffalo, toward mountains where the tribe once went each summer to pick berries and cut lodgepole pine for their tepees. There was no longer war with enemy tribes, no chance to prove one's mettle as a warrior. The religious ceremonies that assured the Cheyenne of their strength were either suppressed or forbidden outright. Other American minorities struggling to assimilate were usually out of sight of their past lives, and there might have been mercy in that.

That Julia Tuell shows in her work a deep appreciation for all aspects of Cheyenne (and later, Sioux) life and culture makes her a woman ahead of her time. Even ceremonies such as the Sun Dance, one of those so feared and misunderstood by Indian agents and the U.S. government that it was outlawed, drew Mrs. Tuell's respect and interest, and she documented them whenever the opportunity arose. Importantly, the people involved trusted her enough to allow her to set up her heavy camera close to very sacred ceremonies. (This was not a day when one could snap candids on the sly with a tiny pocket camera.)

P.V. and Julia Tuell frame their Cheyenne students by the log schoolhouse at Lame Deer, 1907.

In 1912 the Cheyenne experience of Julia and her family ended because of that common hazard of government service, the transfer. P.V. Tuell was assigned to teach among the Sac and Fox Indians at Stroud, Oklahoma. The Tuells and their three children stayed there just one year. Varble recalls discussions of the experience later, recalls his parents saying they did not like the climate in Oklahoma. But it is hard to miss the interesting parallel with the Cheyenne people they had come to know so well, who just a few years earlier had been moved to the south only to long for the north. Was the climate really the problem, or did the Tuells miss the dry, clear air and the big sky, the endless view to the eastern horizon toward Bear Butte, the Bighorns to the south and the Pryors to the west? Was it the scent of sage or maybe the smell of the pines

Northern Cheyenne girl, a student at the log school. The beadwork on her moccasins and leggings is particularly elegant.

in the coulees that made them, like the old woman described by John Stands In Timber, want to go north again?

Mr. Tuell applied for a transfer, but to no avail. Frustrated, he knew but one way to beat the system. He resigned from service, waited a respectable interval, then reapplied to take an opening on the Rosebud Reservation in south-central South Dakota. The Tuell family departed on their own journey to what they now considered home, the north country, this time to a reservation of the Lakota. At this point Julia was just twenty-seven years old. The Tuells would live among the Sioux until 1929, the year P.V. Tuell retired at age seventy after a total of fifty-two years of teaching.

Thus Varble, the youngest of the Tuell children, the purveyor of his mother's legacy, was born on November 23, 1913, on the Rosebud Reservation, east of the Black Hills, in South Dakota. An early snowstorm was raging, and a neighbor lady named Mrs. Clayton, a German, delivered him. ("She must have done a good job," Varble told me, "because I'm pretty healthy." Healthy? Today, at eighty-two, Varble is absolutely *youthful*.) The Sioux called him Nadasha, because of his red hair.

The Tuells' experience with the Sioux (primarily the Brulé tribe of the Teton Lakota) involved three separate schools on the sprawling reservation. Their first was Ringthunder Day School (until 1916), then the day school at Wood, South Dakota, and finally, from 1925 until 1929, the Blackpipe Day School at Norris, South Dakota. The Ringthunder and Blackpipe

Northern Cheyenne school girls in front of the log school at Lame Deer.

schools contained living quarters for the Tuells, while the teaching position at Wood furnished them with a fine home, built by A.K. Wood, a West Virginian for whom the town was named.

Upon arrival at the Rosebud Agency, Julia appears to have hit the ground running. Her photo output resumed, her approach to Sioux culture seeming to be as expansive as it was with the Cheyenne. These were the years of her maturity, the years in which she apparently took normal domestic duties completely in stride while seeking additional challenges. She had, after all, four children from age eleven on down. No further explanation of those challenges

P.V. Tuell in the brick home at Lame Deer, 1910. Note gray wolf rugs on floor, gramophone to right. Already, corner table is adorned with Julia's Cheyenne portraits.

is necessary. She taught at each school (along with her husband) curricular matters called, in those days, "housekeeping." (We would say home economics.) She also came to be a field nurse. Varble explains that the agency did furnish such a nurse, but the work load, particularly during emergencies such as the influenza epidemic of 1918, was overwhelming. Julia assumed the additional duties.

School life alone would have been a handful for most couples. There was no separate staff to clean and maintain the building. All lighting was by kerosene, meaning lamps to be filled and wicks to be trimmed. Heating was by coal, hauled from the railheads by the Sioux with teams and wagons. Any water used had to be pumped by hand and hauled in buckets. Privies, of course, were

A visit to Lame Deer's Tomb, 1906. Lame Deer, a Sioux chief, was killed in a fight with General Miles in 1877.

outdoors. Varble can remember clothes hung to dry on freezing days and the admonition given to children not to touch them lest they snap.

But the twentieth century was marching on, too, and a few years after Varble was born Henry Ford's first marvel came to the Tuell family. Here we'll defer to Varble's narrative but with this explanation: Varble is a car person who collects classic Ford Mustangs. That he should characterize his mother's pioneer spirit by her experiences with an automobile is particularly appropriate. The brand name of Varble's preferred cars is the same as Julia's first one, and we can bet Varble's first ride, at three, started something.

A short time after my parents moved to Ringthunder, South Dakota, in the late summer of 1913, they bought a buggy and a beautiful team of sorrel horses with which they traveled around the Rosebud Sioux Reservation. This was similar to the mode of travel they used in previous years among the Cheyenne Indians from 1906–1912.

A portrait from the year in Oklahoma. Bessie Wakolee of the Sac and Fox, Stroud, Oklahoma, 1912.

Ringthunder Day School on the Rosebud Sioux Reservation in South Dakota, 1912, the first of three schools the Tuells manned after their return to the north. P.V. Tuell and his youngest son, Varble, are on porch at center.

After being transferred to Wood, South Dakota (on the same reservation), in 1916, my father traded the team of horses to Mr. Strain, an auctioneer of that area, for a 1917 Model T Ford car, a touring car which had a canvas top that could be taken off or folded down. Dad was not very mechanically minded, and mother was the pioneer. She took over the job of operating that mechanical toy. This was her way of traveling all over the reservation and all over the state.

If a tire went flat or had to be taken off and patched, Mother was the one who did it. The tire was removed in the field, for there were no spare tires in those days. She would take the tire off the wheel with two tire wrenches. These were very large wheels, thirty inches in size with tires three-and-a-half inches wide, which looked like oversize bicycle tires. When the tire was removed, she had to find the puncture and patch it with a cold patch. This involved scraping the tube with a device made for that purpose, kept in a little repair kit. After scraping to rough up the rubber tube a type of glue was put on the scraped puncture for the patch and let dry. Then she had to put the tire back on the

Julia's children at the Ringthunder School in 1915. From left, Varble, Carl, Julia Mae and Wenonah.

Life at Ringthunder, 1914. Wenonah boosts Carl to get the mail.

Julia shooting her .22 Winchester repeating rifle near Ringthunder, 1914.

wheel and pump it up with the tire pump, then put the wheel back on the car, which, of course, was on a car jack of that day. This was quite a job for a woman who weighed only ninety-eight to a hundred pounds.

These old Model T's had for their transmission three bands, one for forward, one for reverse and the brake band. The bands were concealed in the transmission under a plate on top, which had to be removed in order to adjust them. These were just some of the things that had to be done in order to drive and maintain a Model T. They had no self starter, so they had to be cranked by hand, which was no easy job for someone her size. There were no batteries in those old Fords—they ran on a magneto box under the so-called dash. There were two levers mounted on the steering post just under the steering wheel. One was the gas lever for the carburetor and the other was the spark lever off the magneto box which gave the spark to start the car.

When cranking these old T's the spark lever had to be in about the right position or it would cause the motor to kick back in reverse. If you were cranking and had your hand in the down position it could kick back and break your arm. Most people would pull up on the crank for this reason. There was also a wire choke that extended in front, and you had to pull on this choke the same time you were cranking, which kept both hands busy at the same time.

Of course there were no roads across the high plains of South Dakota, only deep-rutted wagon trails. All highways were dirt graded. Only the main highway across South Dakota from east to west was gravel part way. (Today it is I-90.) A lot of those old wagon trails over the hills and draws were so rough and steep that in order to climb up the hills you had to put your old Ford in reverse. The reason for this was that the gas tank was mounted under the front seat and they had no fuel pumps to force the gas forward into the carburetor, just gravity, and by backing up the gas could run that way.

These were real pioneer days and the old Model T Fords were built for that day. They were high enough off the ground with those large wheels to clear the high centers of the old wagon ruts. Other models of cars were built too low

The Tuell home at Wood, South Dakota, 1916, a spacious home built by A.K. Wood after whom the town is named. Wenonah sits on the rail, Julia Mae on the rocker and their father on the steps.

Julia E. Tuell, photographer at work, 1916, clearing brush for a portrait of John Fast Horse, who appears to smile at the meticulous preparation.

The resulting portrait of Sioux Chief John Fast Horse.

Varble Tuell, age 8.

even in those days to navigate the old country roads of the time. From the horse and buggy to the Model T was a great improvement. It was a little faster (forty miles per hour, top speed), good for that day.

Mother was a pioneer woman and nothing got in her way if she wanted to go out and photograph. She was more or less a perfectionist and artist. She had no fear of rattlesnakes or such as she walked through all that high prairie grass.

Tuell grandchildren in front of the third of the Sioux schools the Tuells tended, the Blackpipe Day School, 1927. The district's name came from a local black stone used to make pipes.

Blackpipe students at P.V. Tuell's retirement ceremony, 1929.

Julia and grandson in front of the Blackpipe Day School during the late 1920s. Varble recalls, "The steeple bell was rung at 8:30 am each school morning, as classes started at 9:00. Recess was at 10:30 and again at 2:30, with school out at 4:00. Some of the little Sioux children rode from as far as five or six miles on horseback or on wagons on cold winter mornings; in sunshine or through South Dakota blizzards, they managed to get to school."

Summer 1927, Norris, South Dakota. Julia's grandchildren, Jack Brown (baby) and June Wheeland with "Quick Bear," Sioux, mowing wild prairie hay for government school use. Blackpipe Day School behind team and mower.

Julia Tuell as a field nurse (with the 1917 Model T Ford described by Varble), working on the Rosebud Sioux Reservation during the 1918 influenza epidemic.

I've always said if a rattlesnake would have been there she would have photographed it also (which she did once as a matter of fact, and I have the picture to prove it).[4]

The Tuells' experience with the automobile was a universal American one. Julia, we remember, was one generation younger than her husband, and the first drivers were young people, just as many of today's youngsters have catapulted ahead of their parents on computer keyboards. My own father-in-law became the family's designated driver at age twelve, when his father's "whoa" failed to keep the new car out of the ditch. But Varble's admiration of his mother's mastery of the Model T is appropriate, for her experiences show how alien to her was any concept of limitation because she was female. We sometimes stereotype and underestimate those who came before us, wrongly assuming that all women were once stifled by customs thrust upon them.

Homesteaders in Mellette County, South Dakota, 1915. Those, like Rolvaag's Per Hansa in *Giants in the Earth*, who came to till the soil and make their homes, changed the face of the prairie forever.

Cowboy near Lame Deer, ca. 1907. Some of the more perceptive Indian agents realized the Sioux and Cheyenne were more suited to cattle raising than to farming; many members of both tribes became cattlemen and still are today.

Characterizations of the western frontier as a man's world exclusively are wrong-headed. The Turner thesis, the idea that the frontier served as an outlet for the restless energy of a growing nation, is equally valid for women if it is valid at all. Julia Tuell, had she stayed east of the Mississippi, may not have had the freedom to charge unaccompanied around the desolate hills of a huge Indian reservation, kicking up dust with her Model T, camera on the seat beside her. But she went west, did have that freedom, and she made the most of it.

Nor was the role of the Native American women she photographed a passive one. Indeed in many ways women were the prime movers of their tribal bands. A Crow woman once slyly related how the women got her village to move. When the campsite began to suffer from overuse of the ground, when the distance firewood had to be carried became intolerable, several of the older

In the Blackpipe district of the Rosebud Reservation, Julia, now in a 1925 Ford sedan, nursing, doing missionary work, attending Eastern Star activities and, as always, taking photographs.

women would simply march over to the chief's tepee and begin to take it down. The rest of the village, seeing this dismantling, took it as a signal and followed suit. Soon the Crow band was on the march to a new location. As the next chapter will show, much of the spiritual power of Plains Indian tribes was also distinctly feminine.

The Tuells lived with the Sioux through World War I, through the plush times in the 1920s, until the year of the Stock Market crash. The old ones among the Sioux, those who could remember a free Plains existence, were gradually dying off. The Custer battle slipped a half-century back in memory, and the country around the reservations in the Dakotas and Montana completely filled with homesteaders, many part of that tide of European immigration that occurred during the first decade of the century. The homesteaders, unlike the mountain men, miners, soldiers and cowboys, did not come to do their thing and then depart; they came to till the soil and to make their permanent homes. The changes in the life of the Plains Indians were now truly irreversible. "All the kings horses and all the kings men . . . " the rhyme goes, and no forces, political or otherwise, could put the Great Circle of Sioux life back together again. The last attempt to do so had been the Messianic fervor of the late 1880s, when Plains tribes had dreamed of a Christ-like figure who would restore their way of life. That hope had died at Wounded Knee.

The need to preserve the culture around her must have been even more pressing to the lady with the camera, and Julia continued her work through World War I, when young Sioux men, adapting their latent warrior natures to the demands of a new kind of war, joined the U.S. military and fought on the battlefields of France. Tepees and tents continued to be adorned with tribal symbols, but also with American flags, as strong feelings of patriotism toward the United States as the Native Americans' own country swept the reservations. (In all the twentieth-century wars with U.S. involvement, Native Americans have been represented in the American military in percentages of population far exceeding the national average.)

As an artist, Julia Tuell did not want to stop at producing first-rate photographs; she wished to exhibit them as well. A piece of writing is incomplete until it has a reader, and a photograph is unfulfilled until it has a viewer. Her remote location was not conducive to recognition by any academic community, but there were notable successes. A photograph and poem by Julia appeared in the May 1913 issue of *Outdoor Life* magazine. (Julia wrote verse, primarily dealing with the tribes she photographed, in a beautiful script.) She tried her hand at fiction, drafting a novel in the Zane Grey genre, beautifully illustrated by her son Varble, in his early teens. *The American Indian Magazine* featured her photo "Evening in Camp" on the cover, with several more inside. Of most lasting importance, perhaps, was an association formed with George Bird Grinnell, the great scholar who spent much of his life studying the Cheyennes, and his wife, Elizabeth, also a photographer.

It is difficult to trace the development of this association, but it is certain Julia Tuell met the Grinnells, probably in 1911 when they were on the Northern Cheyenne reservation to observe a Massaum ceremony. John Stands In Timber, the great historian of the Cheyenne tribe, recalled the occasion:

> I was working in Birney as a line rider for the government at that time, and not collecting many stories, but I remember that at the 1911 ceremony the anthropologist George Bird Grinnell was right in with the medicine men, taking notes. He later wrote it up in a book called *The Cheyenne Indians*.[5]

The result of this happy association was the use of a few of Julia Tuell's photographs in *The Cheyenne Indians* (along with those of Elizabeth Grinnell),

Julia between two of her students during school year 1928–1929 when she was matron of the Rosebud Indian Boarding School with some three hundred girls enrolled. On the right is Nellie Star Boy (Nellie Meynard), who became a distinguished Native American representative, traveling to Washington and becoming acquainted with Eleanor Roosevelt. She still resides on the Rosebud Reservation in South Dakota, and her assistance is acknowledged in Paul Dyck's *Brulé: The Sioux People of the Rosebud*.

with due credit given. Beyond that professional outlet, however, Julia's photographs have not been widely published. A few have appeared on postcards that Julia made herself and sent to friends. (Others have appeared on postcards incorrectly attributed.) Several were copyrighted, but for the most part, when a Tuell photograph has been reprinted its use has been unauthorized. Artists have reproduced several of Julia Tuell's masterpieces in oil with no acknowledgment of the source. Several of these paintings have won critical acclaim. (If any of the photographs in this book look familiar to the reader, this use is the most likely explanation.)

Though copyrighting some of the photographs certainly suggests Julia understood their possible future value, she seems to have been exceedingly generous with them. She gave prints of some to reservation museums, for instance, and to the families of the subjects. The Museum of Men in San Diego, California, has a Tuell collection on display, and the Southwest Museum in Los Angeles has several of Julia's photographs, acquired as part of the Grinnell collection, willed to the museum.

But while it is safe to say that Julia Tuell devoted much of her life to capturing the images in this book, she did not devote similar effort to publishing them. I suspect her life was simply too full to allow that. She raised four children in pioneer circumstances, where water had to be hauled and clothes washed by hand. Her home during most of her productive years was on remote Indian reservations far from the city streets where publishing companies are found. She nursed the sick. She did missionary work. She rose to the position of Worthy Matron in the Order of the Eastern Star and met and photographed its founder, Robert Morris. She became matron of the Rosebud Indian Boarding School, a girls' school with some three hundred students, serving in that position in 1928 and 1929.

P.V. Tuell died in 1942 having lived over forty years in each of two different centuries. He was born on the eve of the Civil War. He had known Frank James, of outlaw fame. Julia lived until 1960. Their last years were spent in retirement in Southern California, far from the land of the Sioux and the Northern Cheyenne.

In the mid–1940s Varble belonged to a flying club in California. Julia had never flown, but wished to. "I want to go out over the ocean," she said. Varble talked to the man he considered the best pilot in the club and asked him to pick a clear day for the adventure. And so four of them—Varble, his sister Wenonah, the pilot he trusted with his mother as passenger and Julia

P.V. Tuell (1859–1942), who retired at age 70 with a total of fifty-two years of teaching.

Varble (left) with Sand Crane and Varble's nephew Raywyn on a journey home with his mother and sister in the fall of 1942. Julia wished to see the north country, the Rosebud and Cheyenne Reservations, again.

Tuell—rose in a Stinson airplane and headed out over the sea.

"And you know what?" Varble told me. "She was *still* taking pictures, this time with a little Argus 35mm she had bought, and she asked us to bank steeply over the ocean so she could get some good ones."

And then there was another ride, a decade later when Julia was nearing seventy, in a new military jeep that Varble was very proud of. The two of them dashed out over the Mojave Desert, the route lengthening beyond what Varble intended, over rutted trails and dry washes. Varble was enjoying himself too much to recall until late in the ride that Julia had been complaining of pains caused by her arthritis. Then he became worried that he had overdone it.

"I thought I must have caused her some pain," Varble told me, "so I asked her if the ride had been a little too much for her arthritis."

"What arthritis?" she asked her son, smiling. "I don't have any. You bounced it all out of me!"

There was a spirit in Julia Tuell that only some people have. Varble's constant explanation for it is, "She was a pioneer woman." Yes, a pioneer woman and an artist and a good person. Some sixteen-year-old brides at the turn of the century would have suffered culture shock with the move from the parlors of Kentucky to a reservation in Montana. Julia's reaction was to feel the precious nature of the culture around her, to see with clarity that it was passing by, its beauty that of the crocus and bitterroot, wildflowers on the prairie that wilt soon if picked and brought inside. But her camera let her freeze for us what could be preserved no other way. The fact that most of her photographs have remained unpublished until now spices them even more, for they are an unopened present, a discovered treasure. And if we have learned anything through the checkered events of the twentieth century, perhaps, now nearing the end of it, we are better able to see what Julia herself saw through that lens, to appreciate what she appreciated, and to love what she so obviously loved.

2 THE WOMEN

BEFORE VCRS, VIDEO GAMES AND the Internet, few American children grew up without imaginary games of "cowboys and Indians." In my particular South Dakota backyard, playing an Indian chief or fearless brave was slightly more prestigious than impersonating a John Wayne character, though both were impressive. (The mortality rate for the chief was higher, but somehow it seemed worth it.) On the rare occasions girls were involved in our games, they invariably put on their most masculine faces and pitched right into roles as Indian braves. It was almost as if in our imaginations Native Americans had come in just one sex. The Noble Savage was decidedly male.

Superficially, this bias may seem to have faded, since I write this in the year following the hit movie *Pocahontas*. But has it? In the film, that character—animated now, larger (and probably more voluptuous) than in life—is romanticized across the screen with little regard for the realities of her historical counterpart. Those of us who live in the Yellowstone River basin are rather more taken with Sacajawea, the young wife of a French interpreter, who guided Lewis and Clark and whose life is somewhat better documented. She was part of a federal government expedition of which President Jefferson himself required reports, so we have a fair amount of information. Her life did result in at least one massive contemporary novel, but with results no more fortunate than the film about John Smith's reputed savior.

In first-rate fiction we do somewhat better. Teal Eye, the little Blackfeet girl with the huge eyes in A.B. Guthrie's *The Big Sky,* keeps our interest. But the unfortunate fact is still that the American public, when it thinks of great Native Americans, is likely to think in male terms only. Some of this is understandable, of course, the result of male roles in the battles around which so much of history seems clustered. White women, as key frontier players, seem equally neglected, if that is any consolation. Forced attempts to make up the deficiency result in fantasies such as the television series *Dr. Quinn, Medicine Woman,* while truly believable female characters and situations, both real and fictional, lie untouched. (Oh, for a first-rate film treatment of the struggles of Beret in *Giants in the Earth* by O.E. Rolvaag.)

Cheyenne girl, 1906.

Young Northern Cheyenne women, Lame Deer, 1907. "The younger woman on the left wears a painted skin dress, her belt dangle of German silver. The older woman wears a tradecloth dress, the yoke rimmed with dentalium shells. Her woman's breastplate is of hairpipes. Both wear beaded moccasins and leggings."—letter from Father Peter J. Powell to author.

Recognition of this problem is not a new thing. Frank Linderman interviewed the Crow chief Plenty Coups on the lawn in front of his home in Pryor, Montana, in 1930. The result was a wonderful book called *Plenty Coups: Chief of the Crows*. But Linderman, having lived much of his life in very close contact with several tribes, recognized the inequity of telling the story of a chief alone, even a great one like Plenty Coups. He knew that the Crows had matriarchal tendencies, that they traced lineage through the mother, not the father, and that women made many of the tribal decisions (though certain roles, such as fighting and buffalo hunting, were left to the men). When the Crows carried out their running feud with John Johnston (alias Liver Eating Johnson and, more euphemistically, Jeremiah Johnson) it is said that the older women of the tribe lined up the young men and chose the twenty who were to singly, in turn, challenge the huge mountain man. Thus Linderman, knowing the importance of women in that tribe, carried out a parallel interview, the result being a book called *Pretty-Shield: Medicine Woman of the Crows*. Originally published as *Red Mother* in 1932, the book was considered the first biography of a Plains Indian woman.

Woostah (Vo'estaa'e, White Cow and White Buffalo Woman), daughter of Morning Star (Dull Knife), who led his people from the south back to the north country they loved, then survived imprisonment at Fort Robinson and a final battle in 1879. "White Cow, during her maidenhood, was considered a beautiful Indian girl, and was spoken afar as 'the belle and the princess of the Cheyennes.' The title of princess came from her father's chieftainship."
—Julia E. Tuell. Woostah and Julia were good friends.

Mrs. Garneaux, wife of a Sioux policeman at Wood on the Rosebud Reservation, 1916. She wears a cape of dentalium shells. Brought to the Plains Indians by white traders in 1860, dentalium shells were soon in tremendous demand by Plains tribes who used them for capes, crowns, earrings and necklaces, worn by both men and women. Note the cross on her necklace.

Fanny One-Feather, Sioux, born in 1905. This photograph was taken in the early 1920s. Varble Tuell visited her sixty years later.

In his foreword Linderman sheds some additional light:

> Throughout forty-six years in Montana I have had much to do with its several Indian tribes, and yet have never, until now, talked for ten consecutive minutes directly to an old Indian woman. I have found Indian women diffident, and so self-effacing that acquaintance with them is next to impossible. Even when Indian women have sometimes acted as my interpreters while gathering tribal legends they remained strangers to me. I had nearly given up the idea of ever writing the life of an old Indian woman when Pretty-Shield delighted me by consenting to tell me her story.[1]

Chief "Kate," Cheyenne.

Sioux women.

We can all be glad of that consent, for the resulting book delights the reader as much as Pretty-Shield's willingness to tell her story delighted Linderman. The book is full of Pretty-Shield's boundless good humor. Her girlhood recollections center on a time when her people still traveled freely, hunting the buffalo and skillfully defending themselves against their many enemies. Like her counterpart Plenty Coups, Pretty-Shield cares little to recall the reservation portion of her life, even though those years were the bulk of it. Indian life as she cared for it had stopped when the buffalo were gone.

Julia Tuell's many photos of Sioux and Cheyenne women at work document them well as the physical backbone of their people, but most of those will be shown in the next chapter. Here we look at portraits more reflective of Native American feminine character. Here are faces that touch the spiritual side of Sioux and Cheyenne women in their most serious roles, those involving birth and life and death.

The central feminine presence in these things was recognized by Native Americans just as it was by the Greeks, who, of course, had Demeter, the goddess of the Earth, the source of all nourishment for its inhabitants. To displease Demeter was disastrous. When Hades, Lord of the Underworld, kidnapped Demeter's daughter Persephone to be his wife, a terrible cold descended on the earth. No grass grew, no birds sang and no flowers bloomed. Neither people nor animals reproduced. The ice was broken only when Zeus worked out his famous compromise, the one the Greeks believed gave us winter

and summer, the sunshine and growing season corresponding with Persephone's half-year return, the cold, short days of winter to her absence.

In *Sweet Medicine,* Father Peter J. Powell illuminates the two great "living, life-blessing covenants" of the Cheyenne, the Mahuts (four sacred arrows), the symbol of male power, and the Is'siwun, the Sacred Buffalo Hat, symbol of female power (spelled Maahotse and Esevone, respectively, in the new Cheyenne language orthography). Both suffered desecration during the nineteenth century, the arrows when stolen by the Pawnees, and the Buffalo Hat when one of its horns was ripped off in a fit of anger by the Keeper's wife. Both desecrations caused the Cheyenne nation terrible distress, and the parallel of the second to Demeter's wrath is difficult to miss.

The word "is'siwun" (esevone) means a herd of buffalo. However, in the context of the Sacred Hat the term also means a group of female bison. The Buffalo Hat is formed from the horned scalp of a female buffalo, and traditionally Is'siwun's power guaranteed a plentiful supply of buffalo for the people. In this power to renew the herds the Hat is linked to the Sun Dance and the Buffalo ceremony. A woman, usually the wife of the pledger of the ceremony, played a vital part in both these ceremonies, for she offered herself in the role of

Sioux woman, White River Frontier Days, early 1920s.

the symbolic reproducer of the tribe, the family, the buffalo, and of creation as a whole.

Consequently, the Sacred Hat is the animate symbol of female renewing power. If the Buffalo Hat is desecrated, there is danger that woman's power will be broken or destroyed. When this happens there can be no new Cheyennes nor any new animals or plants upon which the people can subsist and increase.[2]

The modern public's rather limited knowledge of the Sun Dance is almost exclusively of the male role as detailed in fictional works such as Dorothy Johnson's "A Man Called Horse," the fine short story made into film with Richard Harris in the title role. Depending on the tribe, the male pledger underwent severe physical trials, usually involving skewers through his breasts or back, then either his hanging by thongs attached to them or his pulling desperately against a sapling or buffalo skull until the flesh gave way. Sometimes, after intense effort for many hours failed to break the flesh, assistants would help out with their knives. The female role was known (but not understood) by early reservation officials, however, and, along with the torture endured by the man, was considered a reason for white officialdom to outlaw the ceremony. Had the whites known the enormity of the Sacred Woman's sacrifice in a Northern Cheyenne culture that revered chastity, that had severe rules governing sex and marriage, they might have had some perception of the Sun Dance's power. Both the male and female roles involved sacrifice of something precious in order to renew the power not just of the individuals involved, but of the entire tribe.

Plains Indian women lived with social rules and regulations at least as structured as their white counterparts. Sexual mores varied from tribe to tribe, those of the Cheyenne being quite strict (we might be tempted to erroneously call them Victorian), those of the Crow considerably more liberal.

Chastity was so prized among the Cheyenne that it sometimes did not abruptly end with the wedding night, according to George Bird Grinnell in the work illustrated by his wife and Julia Tuell:

> After a girl had been married and had gone to her husband's lodge, she might still make use of the protective string [a chastity device worn since puberty] for a period of from ten to fifteen days. The husband would respect the string for that length of time, but usually no longer. The Cheyennes say that this custom had the advantage of enabling the newly married couple to get used to each other, to sleeping together. Men tell me they used to lie awake all night, talking to their newly married wives.[3]

In an age when the friendship so crucial to marital relationships is often given short shrift in popular culture, such customs may strike us as wise. However, a period reserved for the couple to become acquainted may have been especially needed, for in many tribes girls had little choice in marriage, the suit for their hand having been plied upon their fathers and other relatives with gifts, usually horses. Often such courtships were quite long, but the level of direct contact between the young man and woman varied considerably from tribe to tribe.

Northern Cheyenne courtship as described by Grinnell in 1923 bears special mention, particularly since Julia Tuell had the foresight to photograph the similar Sioux version for us. Grinnell says the custom was considerably more intimate and informal than older courting rituals that prevailed among the Cheyenne before this newer routine was imported from the Sioux. The young woman in this scenario does have first choice in accepting and rejecting suitors:

> In modern times the young Cheyenne lover did his courting in the old-fashioned Sioux manner. When he became fond of a girl, he went near to the lodge in which she lived, and, wrapped in his blanket or his robe, which was over his head and his features, he stood there, waiting for her to come out. When she passed, on her way to get wood or water, on her return, he stepped up beside her, and threw his arms and his blanket around her, quite covering her person with the blanket. Then he held her fast and began to talk with her. If she did not like this, she broke away from him, and he went away, much mortified; but if she listened to him, he might talk to her for an hour or two— perhaps much longer. If she did not come out of the lodge, he might wait four or five hours, and then go off, to return and try once more.[4]

Grinnell goes on to detail the courtship from there, saying that it traditionally lasted one to five years, that the young man made many gifts of horses to the girl's father during that time. Sometimes, several suitors were wooing the same young woman at once. If special help seemed necessary, the young man might enlist a medicine man to provide him with a special flute, the kind producing tones that could magically persuade the girl in his direction.

Once married, interaction with in-laws was often regulated in some way. Crow men, for instance, were not to look at their mothers-in-law, much less speak to them. If a warrior returned to his lodge while his mother-in-law was visiting, both would avert their eyes while the woman stole away. According to Grinnell, a similar custom prevailed among the Cheyennes. Customs regarding

Sioux courtship, near Ringthunder, South Dakota, 1913. Julia Tuell's note: " . . . In the evenings when all was quiet, it was the custom of the lover to ride to the home of the maiden. Wrapped in his courting robe (almost entirely covered, especially the head and shoulders) he wound his way over the trails, through wild plum bushes, and forded streams. Within hearing distance of the tepee home, he played a soft tune that was selected between them, on a cedar instrument called the flute-horn, similar to our own flute, . . . perfectly formed and neatly decorated with gay ribbons, beads and porcupine quills, [that] had holes burned within them by ordinary iron rods heated in the coals of camp fires. And playing softly the selected tune, the maiden, waiting within her lodge, went out into the night, the moonlight, where, in the shelter of the wild they crooned and mated."

Entitled "The Marriage Ceremony" by Julia Tuell. *Sioux, 1913.* The custom of catching the woman in the blanket was used during courting, then, with a more permanent outcome, during the marriage ceremony itself. " . . . taking the maiden within his same courting robe, he placed her upon his pony and they rode away to some distant place where a lodge had been set for their home, or oftentimes to the home of the lover's parents or relatives, but never to the girl's parents. Three days and nights of living together pronounced them man and wife."—Julia Tuell.

in-laws were made even more complicated by the fact that polygamy was tolerated in most Plains Indian tribes. Normally only warriors who could adequately support more than one wife took a second. Often, the second wife was a sister of the first and normally occupied a separate lodge.

The premium placed upon chastity by the Northern Cheyennes carried over into the marriage as well and affected the intervals at which children were born. Both Grinnell and Powell tell us that a pregnancy shortly after the wedding was common, but that the couple then often waited seven years or longer to have their second child. The long gap between the first and second was considered evidence of restraint and admired.

Babies were nurtured with their mother's milk, held constantly close to that mother's warmth essential for survival. When several months old, children were lashed to baby boards, which made tending and carrying them more practical. The board could be stood against the lodge so the child could have some sun and carried on the mother's back when the tribe was on the move. But in spite of the extreme attention paid to Plains Indian babies, survival was still a struggle. The Cheyennes told Grinnell that many of the babies born in winter during earlier times died.

Pretty-Shield, the Crow, gave Linderman a fascinating account of the birth of her first baby:

> We Crow women had no trouble when our babies were born. I will tell you everything about it. . . . everything was so different when I was young. I was expecting a baby, of course, but was not worrying about it. One day while playing with some girlfriends I felt a little, quick pain, and sat down, laughing about it. One of my friends guessed what was about to happen and told my mother.
>
> But when my mother and a wise-one, named Left-hand, came after me I did not wish to go to the lodge with them. "Yes," my mother urged, "come. We have pitched a new lodge for you, Daughter."
>
> Left-hand's lodge was pitched near my mother's. I noticed now that one of my father's best horses, with several fine robes on his back, was tied there. My father had already paid her for helping me, even before I needed help. Old Left-hand wore a buffalo robe with the hair-side out. Her face was painted with mud, her hair was tied in a big lump on her forehead, and in her hand she carried some of the grass-that-the-buffalo-do-not-eat. Her eyes were so full of fun that I laughed at her as I might have laughed at a mud-clown. And yet she was serious, even solemn in all her actions.
>
> Now I must tell you about the lodge they had pitched for me. Left-hand stopped me just inside the door. A fire was burning, and my mother had made my bed, a soft buffalo robe folded with the hair-side out. This bed was not to lie down on. Crow women do not lie down when their babies are born, nor even afterward, except to sleep when night comes, as others do. Two stakes had been driven into the ground for me to take hold of, and robes had been rolled up and piled against them, so that when I knelt on the bed-robe and took hold of the two stakes, my elbows would rest upon the pile of rolled robes.
>
> While I stood by the door, Left-hand took four live coals from the lodge-fire. One of these she placed on the ground at the door, then one to the left, halfway to the head [center of back—Linderman], one at the head, and one in front of the bed-robe, which was on the right of the door, halfway between it

"A Madonna of the Rosebud." The mother holding the child was Blanch Roubideaux, daughter of Louis Roubideaux, a half-breed interpreter for the Rosebud Sioux Reservation, and his Sioux wife.

Another photograph of *Woostah, White Cow,* holding her granddaughter, at Lame Deer, 1906.

Eva White Cow, daughter of Woostah, granddaughter of Dull Knife, 1907. She holds her baby in a beaded cradleboard. Cradleboards could be tied to the mother's back, carried and propped against lodges when the baby needed sun.

Baby girl of Eva White Cow in cradleboard, 1907.

and the head of the lodge. Then she dropped a little of the grass-that-the-buffalo-do-not-eat upon each of the coals, telling me to walk to the left, to go around to my bed [as the sun goes—Linderman], stepping over the coals.

"Walk as though you are busy," she said, brushing my back with the tail of her buffalo robe, and grunting as a buffalo cow grunts.

I had stepped over the second coal when I saw that I should have to *run* if I reached my bed-robe in time. I *jumped* the third coal, and the fourth, knelt down on the robe, took hold of the two stakes; and my first child, Pinefire, was there with us.

It was always like this in the old days. There must be some reason for the change. I have wondered about it. Perhaps it is because women have grown proud. Yes, I believe this must be the reason.[5]

Pretty-Shield went on to demonstrate to Linderman the kneeling posture she had assumed when giving birth. (She, and Plains Indian culture, did not need Dr. Lamaze to tell them the benefits of gravity during the birth process.) The immediate handling of the newborn and her mother are equally interesting:

I stood up when it was time . . . and then old Left-hand wound a strip of tanned buffalo skin around my waist. After this she greased my baby with grease that had red paint mixed in it, dusting a little powdered buffalo chips [dried manure] and finely pounded clay from its hips down to its knees. Next she put a layer of the hair from a buffalo's head all around the child, and wrapped her in soft buckskin before laying her on a strip of stiff buffalo rawhide to keep her little head from falling backward. After all this was done Left-hand wrapped my baby in tanned calf-skin, and handed her to me. Her work was done, so that she could go about her business.

Each night all this dressing was removed, the baby washed, and again greased, and then left to kick up its heels on a soft buffalo robe until the new wrappings were ready for it. At first we never washed newborn babies. A little later on when they could stand it without danger we washed them every night, the boys in cold water, and the girls in warm water, when we had it. Boy-babies are always tougher than girls.[6]

Plains tribes were exceedingly mobile, the ability to follow the buffalo and to move the village when threatened by enemies having been absolutely essential for survival. Curious how the aftermath of childbirth fit into a lifestyle requiring physical readiness, Linderman asked Pretty-Shield, "But you women did not work for a time after a baby was born to you, did you?"

Northern Cheyenne mother, daughter and grandchildren. Note dentalium shell decoration on the dresses. Lame Deer, 1907.

Oh, yes, . . . But we took short steps when we walked, and ate nothing and drank nothing that was warm, for a whole moon [month]. Besides this, when the village moved and we had to ride, we tied our legs together just above our knees, sitting on flat packs with our babies in our arms, and our feet sticking out in front of us—one foot on each side of the horse's neck. We had to be helped on and off a horse, of course, with our legs tied together, but this did not last longer than one moon.[7]

Plains Indians were exceedingly tolerant parents. Whites, on their first contact with Indian families in the pre-reservation days, were invariably scandalized at what they considered lack of discipline. They were not observing the entire equation, of course, but were quick to note that Native Americans did not hit their children. What psychologists might call "shaping"—approval of

Strong Left Hand (Hote-Ne-A-Ate-Zi), Northern Cheyenne woman, lost her first (of seven) husbands at the battle of the Little Bighorn. She is said to have admitted scalping and mutilating dead soldiers of the Seventh Cavalry after the battle. (Cheyenne dead had met a similar fate at the hands of white soldiers after the Sand Creek Massacre.) Julia Tuell knew her well. Near Birney, Montana, 1906.

good behavior, disapproval of the undesirable—seems to have been practiced, with much of the teaching administered by aunts, uncles and other relatives.

Universal among all the Plains tribes seems to have been a true love for and appreciation of children. Families were often large. Adoption, even of lost or captured members of enemy tribes, was

Strong Left Hand and Cheyenne mother and children with horse travois, 1906.

"A Heavy Pack—A typical scene of the aged Indian carrying home provisions for the younger members of the family after a hard day's toil to earn them. The old woman is Strong Left Hand, a Northern Cheyenne woman from the Montana reservation. She was a participant in the Custer Massacre on the Little Big Horn River in 1876, having lost her first husband in battle. The old woman took part in the scalping of the white soldiers. She has since been married six times, and is the mother of fifteen daughters and two sons. Still lives today, a lovable, jovial old soul, waiting patiently in her rude log hut for her time to travel on into the 'happy hunting grounds' of her people."—Julia Tuell.

Cheyenne girls, Lame Deer, Montana, 1907.

frequent and generous. This trait has carried down to the present day. The local paper I most frequently read (The *Billings* [Montana] *Gazette*) often prints unusually long obituaries for elder members of the two tribes whose reservations are nearby, the Crow and the Northern Cheyenne. The reason for the length is simple: the list of survivors is often incredibly long, filled with both biological and adopted children and grandchildren.

Noting that twins are extremely prominent in Plains Indian mythology, and often figure in creation stories, I once asked a woman whose husband ranched on the Crow and Cheyenne reservations if twins seemed particularly common among the two tribes she knew well. The woman, who was part Crow, thought for a moment, then said that she could not be certain whether there were more twins than among whites, but that twins were by no means unusual. "What I am

Etta Blue Thunder (on horseback) and another Sioux woman before Blue Thunder tepee, Ringthunder, South Dakota, 1913. The beadwork on the horse's bridle, reins and saddle cloth is especially beautiful.

Cheyenne

Old Wool (also Wool Woman and Sweet Taste Woman), Northern Cheyenne, was captured by General Miles's scouts during the bloody year following the battle of the Little Bighorn. "She had slashed her legs with a knife out of grief and sorrow until she needed a cane to guide her."—Julia Tuell, 1909.

"Her Baby's Grave." Northern Cheyenne tree burial, 1907.

sure of," she said, "is that twins are extraordinarily special. It's as if they have something that regular people don't have."

All cultures, it seems to me, reveal when studied great reverence for life, quick as they are to accuse neighboring cultures of lacking such reverence. The Hollywood stereotype of Plains Indians, which shows them swarming into battle with little regard for casualties, was far from true (as we shall see in the next chapter). The truth is, bands of a given tribe were exceedingly small, perhaps just twenty or thirty families, maybe one hundred people. Such a band was like a large, single family that lived together, worked together and fought for survival together. Since infant mortality was high, each child who survived was a future woman or warrior, precious as a pink bitterroot that blooms among the rocks.

And as it fell to Woman to bring into the world the children who would keep her people strong, it fell to her also to mourn their deaths, indeed to lead in the mourning of all death, and to suffer particularly when her husband died. If the death was that of a warrior in battle, his "wife, the mother, and often the sisters, cut their hair short, gashed their heads, and sometimes the calves of their legs, with knives. Sometimes they cut off a finger."[8]

Baby burial in tree. Cheyenne, 1906.

Close view of Indian burial. Cheyenne, 1906.

Box graves, Northern Cheyenne hilltop burial, 1907. "A silent resting place 'mid the pines of the hill tops . . . overlooking vast areas of what was once their hunting grounds, their spots for feasts, dances and tribal ceremonies, these once brave warriors of the West lie peacefully alone and far from the eye of any man. The small can in the foreground shows how . . . members of the family carry food to the graves. Believing the spirit of the dead to return to earth at midnight, hungry, they have there in readiness any manner of food and even cans or pails of coffee that they might partake of it while here. Oftentimes they carry fruit, and even costly beads and other articles."—Julia Tuell.

Julia Tuell holds bow behind Woostah (center) and two more of her Northern Cheyenne friends.

Burial was sometimes on pole platforms in trees, sometimes in caves, and sometimes in a shallow grave covered with rocks. A warrior killed in battle was sometimes left on the ground uncovered, the belief being that it was better for him to be eaten by the coyotes and wolves. Regardless of the method of burial, his finest possessions were often placed with him and his best horse killed nearby.

Women, Grinnell goes on to say, often did not wash the blood from the wounds they gave themselves for some time, and they stayed mourning at the grave, without eating or drinking, so long that relatives had to take them away forcibly. But in the death of her husband, the suffering of a Sioux or Cheyenne woman was not only emotional. In spite of her tremendous importance to the band, a woman's worth was still tied irrevocably to the productive hunter/warrior to whom she was married. When the man died, his lodge was torn down and all his possessions given away. A woman's children went to live with relatives, and she was often left with no more than a blanket to keep her warm. There was mercy for her state, however. A male relative would usually give her a lodge and supply her with meat from the hunt. Eventually her children would return to her, and perhaps, in time, she would remarry.[9] Pretty-Shield told Linderman that among the Crows the seemingly severe customs regarding widows and the old and sick who were unable to travel with the band eased considerably with the advent of the horse and the ability to take along weaker people on a travois.

In studying the female images left us by Julia Tuell, one must look at the faces, at Strong Left Hand who had participated in the horrors of war, at Woostah, whose survival was a miracle separate from the fate of the other children of Dull Knife. There is beauty in the young faces and beauty, too, of a different sort in the character and lines written on the faces of the old. They are, even more than the warriors, the reason their people still live among us.

3 Daily Life

Since the very beginnings of the Romantic Age in the late eighteenth century there has been a tendency to idealize the life of the aboriginal peoples of North America. Around the time of the American Revolution, French and English Romantics seized upon the life of the American Indian as perfection itself and coined the term "Noble Savage." These people, inspired by such philosophers as Jean Jacques Rousseau and Immanuel Kant, had come to the conclusion that human beings were basically good but that civilization was evil. Since all evil germinated not in the human heart but in civilization, a logical step was to declare Native Americans to be the people most untouched by civilization and therefore pure and superior to civilized man.

The Romantic Age's love affair with the native peoples of America proliferated. "The child is the father of the Man," said the English poet Wordsworth. Innocence and virtue were one. Wordsworth's French contemporary Chateaubriand traveled to the United States, the opportunity to see the Noble Savage one of his prime motivators, and did a relatively good job of ignoring the facts about the Native Americans he saw, remnants of eastern tribes already altered by poverty and white man's alcohol. The Romantic ideal suited him better, so he stuck to it by "improving" the tribes he saw in his word pictures of them.

The poet Philip Freneau, writing at the dawn of the American Romantic Age, tells us in a poem called "The Indian Student" of a young lad from "Susquehanna's farthest springs" who, against the advice of a wise priest, goes to college. He studies Greek and Hebrew and is lionized by the institution, which plans to display him: "An Indian savage so well bred / Great credit promised to the schools." But eventually, after the tedium of studies, he sinks into despair:

> And why (he cried) did I forsake
> My native wood for gloomy walls;
> The silver stream, the limpid lake
> For musty books and college halls.

"Moonlight in Dakota." Rosebud Sioux Reservation, South Dakota, 1920. Camp set up for Fourth of July celebration at Wood.

A little could my wants supply—
Can wealth and honor give me more;
Or, will the sylvan god deny
The humble treat he gave before?

Let seraphs gain the bright abode,
And heaven's sublimest mansions see—
I only bow to Nature's God—
The land of shades will do for me.

With that, the student gives up his college gown for his blanket tied with yellow strings, and returns to the forest.

For two hundred years the United States has had a split personality regarding Native Americans. On the one hand, it has idealized them to heights impossible for mere mortals to sustain, while on the other it has persecuted them. (Excuse my cynicism, but while I was teaching I used to postulate for students a hypothetical character who would treat a Native American rudely even while standing in line to plunk his money down for a ticket to see *Dances With Wolves*.) Well, it is not up to me to sit in judgment, but I think the Romantics' picture of the Native American frolicking in the woods or on the prairie, soaking up the bounty of nature, free from the sorrows and complications of civilization, at the very least left out a pretty major chunk of the picture. Living off the land is often viewed as relaxing and carefree, but in truth it entails a staggering amount of *work*.

About this fact, Robinson Crusoe was correct. So was Nathaniel Hawthorne, who against his better judgment briefly lived at Brook Farm, one of the communes based on romantic ideals so popular in the 1840s (and the 1960s). Hawthorne found that after a day of pitching manure in the cow barn he had a great deal of difficulty going to his room and being creative. More than a century later a young marine from northern Michigan came to my desk laughing, insisting I look at something. He showed me an article on people with a back-to-the-land philosophy and a photograph of a couple who had built a rude shack in the Michigan north woods, the homeland of this particular marine. The couple stood in front of the shack next to a stack of firewood perhaps eight feet long and four feet high. The caption read that the young idealists were showing off their winter supply of firewood. The marine, normally quiet, positively guffawed. "Their winter's supply? If they're lucky they'll get two weeks out of it, one week if it's cold!" He knew the young couple simply had no concept of the immense quantity of wood it takes to keep warm through a northern Michigan winter.

Whatever the virtues of life close to nature (and I should add that I personally believe in many of them), such a life is not easy or carefree. Nature, particularly in northern climes, is simply too hard for that. The northern Plains are especially unforgiving. Half the year a biting wind blows, and snow drifts belly deep on the horses. During the free-roaming years of the Plains Indians there were no supermarkets for food; it was all on the hoof, looking out for its own survival by staying away from them, the hunters. The only warmth was from wood cut and burned in the tepees and from the skins of animals taken. There were no modern clinics for medical attention, and no local cavalry for protection if an enemy tribe proved overwhelming.

Although trade existed, almost everything had to be made: clothing, moccasins, bows and arrows and saddles. And before such things could be made the very materials used had to be acquired from nature and prepared. Moccasins meant that an animal had to be killed, its hide scraped and tanned (using the acids from the brains and internal organs), cut to shape, then sewn, perhaps with a bone needle. (And, of course, that bone came from another animal.) A sinew which lay along the backbone of a deer or antelope was required for a bow string, and the right birds had to be taken to feather the arrows. Again, it added up to work, a great deal of it. There was division of labor in this, the men having their tasks, the women theirs, and from the beginning whites had difficulty understanding the division. It appeared to them that most of the work was performed by the Indian women. William Byrd II, writing in the early 1700s, stereotyped the male Indian as one who made his poor wife do all the work. That did appear to early whites to be the case, but they misunderstood what they were seeing. Learning that the male did the hunting, European aristocrats jumped to the conclusion that the men were having all the fun, since hunting in Europe by the upper classes was a sport. Nor did they understand that the warriors needed to be unencumbered during tribal moves, free to quickly react and defend the column if attacked. Thus, the warrior's horse carried no additional pack, while those of the women were heavily laden.

Among the Cheyenne, according to George Bird Grinnell, " . . . woman was an equal partner with man, and the division of duties which existed between the sexes appeared in their industries. The men usually made men's utensils and weapons, and many of the ceremonial implements, while women provided the articles used in the household as well as the dwelling, the family clothing, and the cooking utensils."[1]

Angela Porcupine fastening the split sticks on her lodge door, Northern Cheyenne, 1908.
Mrs. Porcupine's husband was the priest who introduced the Ghost Dance among the
Northern Cheyennes and was a Sun Dance priest.

The basics of survival anywhere include shelter, food, clothing and, in the case of a nomadic people, transportation. Approaches to each of these evolved among the Plains Indians organically, in ways perfectly suited to their environment and the resources at their disposal. We think of the tepee as a traditional Plains Indian dwelling, perhaps without reflecting on how well it suited the needs at hand. First, it was portable, a requirement for mobile people. The poles came from a type of pine found on the eastern slopes of the Rocky Mountains, a tall, slim tree with few branches except at the very top.

This pine still bears the name of its traditional use—lodgepole. Periodically Plains Indian villages would move to the mountains to cut a supply of this ideally suited tree. During village moves, the same poles that held up the lodges became the travois dragged behind horses (dogs pulled smaller versions) to form

A less romantic view. An old (and apparently poor) Cheyenne woman holds her grandchild, 1906.

Rosebud Sioux Reservation, Ringthunder district, 1913. Dressed for a celebration.

Reservation-era camp, Northern Cheyenne, ca. 1908. Canvas gradually replaced buffalo hides for tepee construction, and some Cheyennes used army-style wall tents.

a platform on which a considerably greater load could be hauled than could be packed on the animal's back. The travois also carried children too small to walk or ride horseback.

The skin of the tepee was traditionally buffalo hide, though the hides of smaller animals could be used. Buffalo hide is extraordinarily strong, but also heavy. Most tribes embraced the canvas available from traders as a lighter substitute for bison hide, so many tepees came to be made from that material even before the buffalo disappeared.

The shape of the tepee is "form follows function" epitomized. First, the conical shape shed snow and rain efficiently, with sides steep enough to prevent accumulation of heavy snow. Secondly, the shape spilled the wind when it howled across the prairie, letting the structure stay standing through vicious

Julia Tuell with her daughters and baby Carl at Lame Deer, 1909.

storms. Thirdly, the tepee's form was suited to a central fire inside, producing a natural chimney effect that could be regulated with the movable smoke flap.

Tepees were sometimes lavish to the point of luxury. Like the Bedouins on the other side of the globe, the wealthiest among Plains Indians mastered the art of making their portable homes comfortable. Inner liners both trapped air for insulation and, beautifully painted with war and hunting scenes, furnished color to the interior. Buffalo robes, taken when the animals had their longest, softest winter coats, floored part of the inside with a warm and comfortable layer. Roll-up mattresses made of willow provided insulation and comfort for sleeping.

Snow banked around the outside of the lodge prevented air infiltration under the skin of the tepee. When food and firewood supplies were adequate, the Cheyenne and Sioux wintered well indeed. But this comfort was bought with endless hours of physical labor tanning and preparing the hides and robes, then sewing it all together with sinews for thread.

It has been said that an army moves on its stomach, and the saying applies equally to the mobile villages of the Plains Indians. The diet of the Cheyenne and Sioux changed with their moving from the upper Midwest to the Great Plains. Certainly their earlier diet was more complex. As farmers they had planted such staples as corn and squash, and for meat had harvested the many smaller animals common to the Midwestern woodlands: rabbits, squirrels and an occasional deer. Their eating habits changed drastically with the coming of the

Tepee interior, Northern Cheyenne, Lame Deer, ca. 1908. Depending on the wealth of the family and the times, tepee interiors ranged from spartan to extremely comfortable.

"Homeward Bound." Lakota (Sioux) with horse travois returning to camp, Rosebud Agency, September 1918. Lodgepoles could double for travois when villages moved, and the device allowed the transporting of small children and bulky items.

horse and their move west. They became the predator that occupied the top of the food chain, and their primary diet was meat, red meat, with bison the highest priority.

The buffalo hunters did not, of course, give up everything else in their diet. The tribes continued to plant an occasional vegetable when the prospect existed of returning to a particularly fertile campsite at harvest time. They dug various edible tubers, and they traveled to the mountains to harvest berries. Grinnell said Cheyenne women spoke of some thirty-five to forty plants that served as food. Many more were sought for medicinal properties. A bush called "red leaf wood" produced leaves which when boiled made a tea similar to sassafras.[2]

In the Dakotas and Montana nearly every coulee in the rolling foothills contains chokecherry bushes. In late August the branches sag with the sour little

View of the dog travois. "The very earliest known travel among the Indians of the northern tribes was by the dog travois. The earliest history of the chiefs show us that as small children, they were strapped securely to the dog travois, and the faithfulness of the dogs guaranteed their safety." —Julia Tuell. Even after these tribes acquired horses, dogs continued to be a useful beast of burden, both dragging travois and carrying packs. This photograph is of Leading Cloud, Sioux, in the Blackpipe district of the Rosebud Reservation, ca. 1920.

A gentle, trusted dog, with Sioux child on the travois, 1925.

red-black berries, and one's hand wrapped around a bearing twig strips off a dozen at a time. The Indian people pounded these into a mash and dried them in cakes. (Drying, of course, was the only means of preservation available to a society without spices or refrigeration.) The dried berries could be mixed with dried, flaked meat and fat to produce the original "trail mix," called pemmican. Portable and high in calories, that mixture kept many a warrior and mountain man hunting through the winter.

But while a vegetable component did exist in the diet of the Cheyenne and Sioux, the vast bulk of their cuisine was red meat. There are records of warriors eating many pounds of meat at one sitting, following this binge with a brief nap, then engaging in tremendous physical exertion, such as setting out on foot at a run to steal horses fifty miles away. This extreme activity might last several days, during which the warriors would not eat. Then the cycle would be repeated. (This scenario was similar to that of another great predator of the Plains, the

Medicine Blanket, a Sioux woman, using a stone mortar and pestle to grind chokeberries that will be flattened into patties and dried, 1926.

wolf.) The white men who traveled west were also caught up in this nearly all-meat diet. Hudson's Bay Company's famous voyagers paddled canoes during summer and trotted behind toboggans pulled by dog teams all winter. Their daily allotted ration, *per man,* was eight pounds of meat or two geese or four ducks!

There is every evidence that before the northern tribes were influenced by civilization's illnesses (and eventually its alcohol) the people were exceedingly healthy. Mark Brown quoted Edwin Denig's early description of the Crows, for

Julia with Medicine Blanket grinding chokeberries.

"In this manner the Indian people cured the buffalo meat following their big hunts, and the custom is still practiced by the Sioux and Cheyenne today. The meat is severed in large pieces, then . . . is sliced . . . to unroll the pieces in lengthy strips . . . about the thickness of usual steak meat. The strips are then placed on long poles . . . to allow the free passage of air between them, and . . . small twigs from the willows . . . are fastened into the strips of meat to fasten them at their widest . . . to allow the sun and air to dry it, or cure it, in a very crisp and even manner. And after storing it away in this jerked condition in rawhide sacks they kept their families supplied with meat all during the long winter months when no hunting was in progress."—Julia Tuell. Cheyenne woman preparing meat to dry on poles, Lame Deer, 1907.

Strong Left Hand drying meat, 1906.

instance: " . . . decidedly prepossessing . . . They are all tall, straight, well
formed, with bold, fierce eyes and as usual good teeth."[3] I assume the "as usual"
regarding teeth means that this was a trait shared by Indians generally, and one
wonders if the lack of sugar in the diet could be an explanation. The usual
diseases of the white man—colds, influenza, measles and the most dreaded one,
smallpox—were unknown until contact with "civilization." Then the results
were devastating, for Native Americans had lived in a pristine environment and
had not built up resistance to even the most minor of the ailments. But nearly all
the oldest people among the Plains tribes recalled to the first white visitors an
age when sickness was virtually unknown. As to reconciling their health and
vigor with a diet dominated by consumption of red meat, we must leave that to
those current dietitians to whom red meat is anathema.

A hunting society operates on the feast-and-famine principle, however. Before scientific game management came to the West, animal populations were extremely cyclical, and they still are to a degree. Lewis and Clark nearly starved in western Montana, for at the time they progressed through that area game was virtually non-existent. At the very least, fresh meat could not be counted upon at neatly graduated intervals, so drying was necessary to build up a winter's supply. The meat was thinly sliced and placed on racks, where the dry western air and the sun would convert it to jerky. Sometimes a smoky fire was maintained under the rack to discourage flies and speed the drying process.

Though the bison was the dominant animal sought, the Plains Indians ate virtually all species. (The white mountain men quickly picked up a "meat is meat" philosophy, eating nearly all varieties and deeming the mountain lion on top of the heap in tastiness.) There was usually no conflict with an animal's spiritual status and its appropriateness as a food source. Hindus hold cows sacred and do not eat their meat, but among the Plains Indians sacred animals were thanked and used. An exception was the white buffalo, a rarity which, if it should happen to be killed, was left lying in place until it could be dealt with in a sacred manner. Most Plains tribes regarded this rare animal as particularly sacred, and special ceremonies and taboos existed concerning its use and the treatment of its robe.

When discussing the day-to-day existence of the Sioux and Cheyenne during their free-roaming years on the Plains from, perhaps, the late 1700s until the reservation era began a century later, we must remember that there were immense differences in approach to nearly all subsistence tasks. It is not so simple as documenting one sort of life before the white man's influence and another after. The question is not whether the white man was of influence, but *to what degree.* The historian Robert Utley has pointed out that, ironically, this free-roaming Plains Indian existence was made possible by a contribution of the white man, since it was Europeans who brought the horse to the New World. By the time the Sioux and Cheyenne were emerging from their woodland existence, life was already altered, sometimes made easier, by items acquired from Hudson's Bay and other white traders.

For instance, it comes as a surprise to many (and is completely unknown to many Hollywood directors) that Plains Indians in the late nineteenth century did not use stone points on their arrows. Innocent souls still search the sites of battles between the U.S. Cavalry and Plains Indian tribes in the hope of finding stone arrowheads. They *may* find such arrowheads in those locations, but with an origin probably a century earlier than the battles in which they are interested.

Moonlight in Dakota, July 4, 1920

Eva White Cow and her baby, the granddaughter of Chief Dull Knife

Fast Horse and wife

Strong Left Hand with
horse travois, 1906

The dog travois, Sioux

The reason is that the earliest white traders sold a hot item to Indian tribes: sheet metal. From it were fashioned far more lethal and effective arrow points than the beautiful ones made of flint.

Indeed, elderly Plains Indians during the late nineteenth century were unable to recall a time when the stone arrowheads were made by their tribes. The origin of the points was considered mysterious among the Crows, who attributed the construction of stone arrowheads to the Little People, tiny mythological folk who occupied a cave network near Pryor, Montana. In any case, the tremendous effectiveness of the warrior's bow on buffalo was partially attributable to its wicked iron point. Often, the hunter drove an arrow completely through the bison's rib cage so that the missile sailed through the other side.

Of course, the whole method of hunting called buffalo running was made possible by the horse. Earlier methods of taking the huge animals had included funneling a herd toward a cliff with fences, then running them over the edge. The animals in front realized their fate too late to prevent the press of those behind them from pushing them off. An immense butchering effort then occurred at the bottom of the cliff.

Buffalo running was both more exciting and more efficient. (In the more primitive method it was impossible to regulate the number of bison taken.) Always done as a group effort, buffalo running involved the warrior's best horse, often reserved exclusively for that purpose. The horse must have had a version of what modern cattlemen call "cow sense," and its training was extremely refined, for it was guided completely by knee pressure from the rider, both of whose hands were occupied by the bow or rifle. The bow was in many ways the better weapon, because it allowed quick repeat shots, unlike the muzzle-loading rifles of the day. Some white mountain men converted to the bow for this reason. The rifle, whether manned by warrior or mountain man, normally was loaded with a cloth patch around the lead ball to engage the rifling, a tight fit, so a ramrod was needed to push the ball down the barrel and seat it on top of the powder charge. Such cumbersome manipulation was impossible aboard a galloping horse. Thus, the patch was eliminated. The hunter dropped a powder charge down the barrel from his powder horn, then spit the ball into the muzzle. Holding the muzzle elevated so the patchless ball would not roll out, he waited until the last moment when his horse was chest-to-chest with the buffalo targeted, then quickly dropped the muzzle and fired before the ball could escape. (Repeating cartridge rifles, arriving near the end of the bison era, eliminated all this, of course.)

After their free-roaming days came to an end, the Plains Indians had to depend upon government rations agreed upon (but not always supplied) in the various treaties. Rationing day on the Northern Cheyenne reservation, Lame Deer, 1906.

Many miles were sometimes covered before the necessary number of bison were killed. A small army of women, children and old people followed the hunt, skinning and cutting up the buffalo. Horses, like buffalo, are herd animals, and most must have gone absolutely wild when participating in this frenzy. The nosie was deafening, as anyone who has witnessed even a small herd of running cattle or horses. Pretty-Shield, the Crow woman, told Linderman:

> Running buffalo was a man's business, anyhow. . . . Everytime that I got mixed up with a buffalo herd I wished myself anywhere else. Good buffalo horses always went wild when they ran after buffalo. Even old pack-horses would sometimes get foolish and think themselves buffalo-runners. . .[4]

Pretty–Shield also relates the story of the day her father loaned her his buffalo horse, a buckskin he normally reserved only for buffalo running and which was not even asked to carry a load when the tribe moved. The horse was pampered, overfed and so gentle any child could ride him—until buffalo were spotted. "A strong man could not hold him once he started after a buffalo." Because such regal treatment was making him too full of life, Pretty-Shield's father thought the horse should get some light use on a tribal move, that the weight of a ten-year-old girl would not harm his pet, so he let Pretty-Shield ride him when the village relocated. Proud of her mount, Pretty-Shield made the mistake of thinking it would be fun to rope one of the calves.

A good cutting horse detects which animal the cowboy is after, then seizes on it with total concentration. Buffalo horses were similar. Pretty-Shield's mount decided which calf the girl wanted to chase and pursued it like a guided missile. Too intent on staying on the back of this buckskin comet that threaded its way through the stampeding herd, Pretty-Shield soon lost interest in the roping project. "I could have touched that calf with my hand, any time, but now I did not want it. Disgusted because I did not shoot, the buckskin horse struck that calf with his front hoof, knocking it down and jumping over it to save himself from falling." At that point Pretty-Shield screamed and her father appeared. "He took the buckskin away from me 'This horse has more sense than you have,' he said. 'He saw that if any meat was going to be killed he would have to do it himself; and then you screamed,' he laughed."[5]

Even non-hunters can understand the terrible deflation of the reservation years when there were no more buffalo to be run. In a feeble attempt to duplicate the experience, steers forming the beef ration furnished by the government were sometimes killed by warriors riding ponies. A family's name was called out and their animals were released, the men riding the bovines down and killing them. Some reservation officials considered the procedure barbaric and stopped it. Many of us, contemplating the domestication of such an exciting wild spectacle, are more likely to deem it, simply, sad. Rationing day, as pictured in this chapter, must have seemed a sorry substitute for the hunt. The slaughter house soon replaced the sham hunt, the beef being butchered and the Indian families receiving their ration of meat.

The tribes considered beef to be inferior to buffalo meat. We know that grass-fed beef, prepared without feeding the animal grain, is virtually indistinguishable, either by analysis or by the palate, from bison meat. But Plains Indians called beef soft meat, because it made one's muscles soft, while buffalo was hard meat, because it did the opposite. Sadly, again, we can speculate that the activity of the hunt made for strong and healthy men, while passively receiving a government ration did not.

Before the reservation era, the Plains Indians did have two domestic animals that could be used for food if needed, the horse and the dog. Grinnell states that the Cheyennes would eat horseflesh but preferred other meat. The horse's value, alone, would be enough to discourage its use for food if anything else was available. The Kiowas, however, apparently relished horsemeat, particularly that of a fat colt, and actually preferred it to bison. As if to make their case more strongly, Grinnell assures the reader that horsemeat is extremely palatable.[6]

The dog was a traditional part of Plains Indian life. Before the horse was available it served as the primary beast of burden, carrying packs and pulling the travois. Even after the tribes acquired the horse the dog remained a useful beast of burden. The village dogs served an important security need as well, sending out a cacophony of barking when strangers approached. (Escaping notice of the village dogs is often mentioned in warriors' descriptions of their pony-stealing raids.)

As food, dogs were a staple. There are many references to white dogs as being reserved for special feasts. Grinnell says that the Cheyenne women killed dogs by strangulation, two women looping slip knots around the animal's neck, then pulling in opposite directions, suspending the animal between them until it died.

The historian Francis Parkman who lived with the Sioux in the 1840s learned, in spite of his blue-blooded Boston background, to relish a dog stew as much as the warriors around him. His description of the butchering of a dog is touching, for the woman involved hardens herself, conditions herself psychologically to accept what she is about to do:

> In front of the lodge . . . a squaw was standing, angrily scolding an old yellow dog, who lay on the ground with his nose resting between his paws, and his eyes turned sleepily up to her face, as if pretending to give respectful attention, but resolved to fall asleep again as soon as it was all over.
>
> "You ought to be ashamed of yourself!" said the old woman. "I have fed you well, and taken care of you ever since you were small and blind, and could only crawl about and squeal a little, instead of howling as you do now. When you grew old, I said you were a good dog. You were strong and gentle when the load was put on your back, and you never ran among the feet of the horses when we were travelling together over the prairie. But you had a bad heart! Whenever a rabbit jumped out of the bushes, you were always the first to run after him and lead away all the other dogs behind you. You ought to have known that it was dangerous to act so. When you had got far out on the prairie, and no one was near to help you, perhaps a wolf would jump out of the ravine; and

Dogs were one domestic animal available to Plains Indians for food. After butchering (usually by strangulation) the whole dog was singed in fire so the hair could be scraped.

then what could you do? You would certainly have been killed, for no dog can fight well with a load on its back. Only three days ago you ran off in that way, and turned over a bag of wooden pins with which I used to fasten up the front of the lodge. Look up there, and you will see that it is flapping open. And now tonight you have stolen a great piece of fat meat which was roasting before the fire for my children. I tell you, you have a bad heart, and you must die!"

So saying, the squaw went into the lodge, and coming out with a large stone mallet, killed the unfortunate dog at one blow.[7]

Once killed, dogs were normally put into the fire whole to singe the hair, which was then scraped. Finally, the meat was cut into small pieces to go into the stew. This custom of eating dogs continued well into the reservation days, perhaps increasing during the many hard times when government-issued rations

Then meat was cut into pieces for dog stew. Rosebud Sioux Reservation, 1916.

Jenny Leading Cloud, Sioux, fetches water from Blackpipe Creek on the Rosebud Reservation, 1926.

fell well short of the quantity agreed upon in the treaties. Varble Tuell remembers that during his boyhood the Sioux would buy litters of puppies and also the carcasses of fur-bearing animals taken on the trapline.

The photographs in this chapter document a hard and busy life. Julia Tuell realized that pictures of tasks such as drying meat and grinding chokecherries and butchering dog were as important as dignified portraits. The early years of the twentieth century were last-chance years for this subject matter as much as they were for capturing on film the warriors who fought Custer. The skills involved in living off the land on the northern plains would wane soon.

But work was not the entire picture. There was play as well. The old folks had their socializing, the young adults their courting, and the children their

Cheyenne women scraping hide in preparation for tanning.

Jenny Leading Cloud stretching and staking out a hide for tanning. Blackpipe
Creek is in background. Rosebud Reservation, 1916.

"The Trapper—this scene is on a beaver dam on the Little White River, Mellette County, South Dakota. This strip of country extends from the river's edge back into the former beautiful camping ground of the Dacotah people . . . The old man is Comes-From-Scout, who still today dwells in his log cabin near the scene. His only son Benjamin was a volunteer in the present World War and gave up his life in the battle of Chateau-Thierry. Just to the north of this scene stands the Bad Lands in their majestic beauty."
—Julia Tuell, written during World War I.

"Little Cheyenne Warrior," Lame Deer, 1907.

dolls and toy bows and arrows. Grinnell devotes a long chapter of *The Cheyenne Indians* to the many complex sports the Cheyennes played, from shooting and wrestling contests to versions of hide and seek. There was a wheel game, involving wheels made of willow sticks sprung into a circle and lashed with a network of thongs. Openings in the wheel signified species of game animals or portions, such as the heart, and spearlike sticks were thrown at the wheels in an attempt to penetrate or "kill" the target.

Little boys had toy tops and girls had a game similar to bowling. In the winter the children slid down snowy hills on hides, often encouraged by their mothers who knew that the wear on the hair side of the pelt would make it easier to scrape later. Some of the games were quite rough. In kicking matches, "The boys and young men kicked each other with one or both moccasin-shod feet, kicking either from the ground, or jumping up in the air and lashing out sideways with both feet. The blows dealt were often severe, yet the contests were always good-natured."[8]

In addition to the play, there must have been many lovely summer nights when the northern sun lingered long and the smell of pine smoke came from the lodges to mingle with that of roasting ribs and, on the western breeze, the scent of sage. The village dogs howled in answer to the coyotes singing on the prairie. Laughter came from the campfires along with exclamations at stories

Cheyenne children at play, 1907. Their toy tepees have designs similar to those on the full-sized tepees of their parents. Writing of her girlhood in the pre-reservation days, Pretty-Shield said, "Once several of us girls made ourselves a play-village with our tiny tepees. Of course our children were dolls, and our horses dogs, and yet we managed to make our village look very real . . ."

told of conquests against enemies and success on the hunt. With one's friends and family in camp, there was a powerful sense of community, the type so hard to find in our modern lives.

Perhaps, after all, the Romantics were more on target than off in their assessment of Plains Indian life, for it is certainly true that civilization crushed many beautiful things, not the least of which was the freedom and self-reliance of these nomadic bands. Just as it is true that large predators such as grizzly bears and mountain lions require huge chunks of real estate to provide enough prey for their support, a relatively small band of Plains Indians was, in effect, a collective predator, a hunter, that required much space, much pristine land, to

"Evening in Camp." Cheyenne children swimming in Lame Deer Creek, named after the Sioux chief killed in a fight with General Miles and buried in a rock outcropping just to the left of this scene. This photograph was on the cover of *The American Indian Magazine,* Summer, 1919.

survive. In this sense, with no intent to justify the terrible treatment of these people by a larger, more powerful society, we can say that maybe the free-roaming existence of the Sioux and Cheyenne was almost too good to be true, was doomed as the world's population of human beings expanded. We are left to wish that it had not been so and to try to live it vicariously.

4 THE WARRIORS

WHEN A CHEYENNE WARRIOR DIED, his body, dressed in its finest clothes, was wrapped in robes or blankets, securely lashed with rope, then deposited in a burial lodge or on the open prairie with little to protect it from the coyotes, wolves and eagles. For predators to use the body was natural and not to be feared. Sometimes burial was in a tree on a platform of poles. Sometimes the body was placed in a natural cave or hole in the rimrocks, the opening then being sealed with rocks to complete the tomb. The warrior's best war implements were placed with him (although a favorite piece of equipment might first be given by his relatives to a good friend), and his best horse was brought nearby, saddled and bridled, then killed for the brave's use after death. Next the warrior's soul would ride until it found a trail where all the tracks pointed one way. This trail would lead him to the Milky Way, which he would follow until he found Seano, the camp in the stars, the camp of the dead, where he could reunite with friends and relatives and begin his afterlife.[1]

Father Peter J. Powell describes Seano as " . . . a pleasant land. Here the Cheyennes of the past live in heaven just as they did upon earth. In Seano, newly arrived souls are reunited with their long-departed loved ones, and all dwell happily, near Maheo Himself."[2]

But I wonder about the Cheyenne concept of a pleasant place. Could the Cheyenne warrior be happy in a place where there was no chance to fight? He took weapons on his trip to the afterlife. Were they only necessary to protect him on a long and treacherous trip along the Milky Way? Or was the concept of existence anywhere inseparable from his warrior tradition?

Among the Plains Indians, a man's identity as a warrior and the importance of battle in his culture were everything. Among the Sioux and Cheyenne a boy was not allowed to court a girl until he had been in battle. (Imagine American culture banning relations with the opposite sex to all males who were not combat veterans.) The Crows seem to have been even more stringent. A young man could not court a girl until he had counted coup in battle or until he reached age twenty-five. (The age concession was probably recognition that battle is fickle, that in spite of one's best efforts the opportunity to touch an enemy could be elusive.)

Northern Cheyenne boy, 1907. "The Cheyenne men were all warriors. War was regarded as the noblest of pursuits, the only one for a man to follow; and from earliest youth boys were encouraged to excel in it. They were taught that no pleasure equaled the joy of battle; that success in war brought in its train the respect and admiration of men, women, and children in the tribe, and that the most worthy thing that any man could do was to be brave."—George Bird Grinnell.

Further evidence of the prominence of war in Plains Indian culture was how much it was missed after the reservation era began. Repeatedly, old warriors would cite the absence of two things as making life meaningless on the reservation: The buffalo were gone and it was no longer possible to make war on their traditional tribal enemies.

Chiefs whose greatest prominence actually occurred after the reservation era began, such as Two Moon among the Cheyenne and Plenty Coups among the Crow, refused to discuss their accomplishments during reservation years. The latter said to Frank Linderman that there was nothing more to tell once the buffalo were gone. He had no desire to relate his trips to Washington to testify before Congress or his friendship with Teddy Roosevelt. These experiences, though lauded by others, were relatively unimportant to him. When World War I began, however, Plenty Coups, like most leaders among Plains tribes, urged the young men to enlist in the U.S. military, to go overseas and renew their warrior tradition by fighting the Germans. Julia Tuell captured a Sioux ceremony for Indian soldiers returning from overseas. "Damn the Kaiser" is emblazoned on a banner, and American flags fly in the breeze.

The warrior tradition continues. Sioux war dance and Fourth of July celebration during World War I. The banner reads, "Damn the Kaiser."

As mentioned earlier, American Indian participation in the U.S. military was significant throughout twentieth-century wars, the percentage of enlistment from most tribes higher than that of the public at large. Most know the story of the corps of Navaho Marines whose radio messages in their language baffled the Germans, defying their best efforts to break what they thought was a code. Codes can be broken but not languages. What many today may not realize is the strength of American patriotism on western reservations. No prouder groups exist in Montana today than organizations of Native American veterans.

Grinnell believed the intense rivalry with other tribes which fueled the warrior tradition was a relatively recent development among the Plains Indians. When the Sioux and Cheyenne were midwestern agriculturists, there was little motivation to make war on other tribes. The horse changed all that. First, it

transformed the tribes into mobile hunting societies (as discussed in chapter 1) and secondly, because of its immense capabilities, the horse became extremely valuable in itself, a living, breathing piece of currency. Although other possessions were cherished, the horse became the center of wealth. A man with many was

Chief American Horse, Northern Cheyenne, 1906. American Horse was chief of the Sotaaeoo band of the Northern Cheyenne, was involved in both the battle of the Rosebud and the battle of the Little Bighorn and steadily gained influence as a spokesman for his tribe during the early reservation years. He cared for tribal funds and put his mark on legal correspondence with Washington. In 1907 American Horse was one of the leaders who successfully petitioned white reservation officials to allow

the return of the Sun Dance. According to George Bird Grinnell, he had also been prominent in the Massaum, having worn the wolf skin before naming Spotted Elk as his successor. American Horse became a good friend of the Tuells during their years at Lame Deer, Montana, on the Northern Cheyenne Reservation. He came to their log cabin frequently for coffee and taught Julia the Cheyenne language. American Horse died in July 1911 at age 83.

Hairy Hand, Northern Cheyenne warrior, prominent in the fight to defend the village of Morning Star (Dull Knife), in which he rescued a fellow warrior in the heat of battle.

A tepee with painted canvas cover depicting a battle, probably between the Cheyennes and a rival tribe such as the Crows or Nez Percés. (Children can be seen peeking out from under the tepee.) Lame Deer, 1907.

wealthy, while a man with few was poor. The stealing of horses from enemy tribes became a way of life.

Thus, earlier warfare between tribes on the Plains did not exist to kill enemies or to conquer their territory but to take their horses. Killing was not glorified, because it was relatively unimportant. The object was to steal into a village at dawn, cut loose the horses and drive them back to the home camp as quickly and cleanly as possible. Open confrontation with the enemy in these situations was a delay, a distraction.

Throughout a century or so of intertribal warfare, the primary way in which one distinguished himself in battle was not to kill and to scalp his enemy but to count coup on him. Depending on the tribe there were several ways of doing this, but counting coup most commonly involved the warrior's touching the enemy with an item he carried—for example, a coup stick, a lance or a ramrod. The enemy could be either dead or alive when coup was counted. In the case of a dead enemy, just who had killed him was immaterial; the warrior who touched him first counted coup. As many as four or five warriors could count coup on the same slain enemy, again depending on the tribe, but the order was remembered and the prestige of the first was greatest. As one would expect, there were sometimes arguments later about who, in the heat of battle, had counted coup in what particular placement.

The ultimate in warrior machismo was not to kill the enemy at all but to ride into his ranks unarmed except for the coup stick, count coup on a live enemy, then retreat. Many accounts of tribal battles relate tales of a particularly brave warrior who did this. As to scalping dead enemies, the Cheyennes told Grinnell they learned this from the Assiniboin tribe in an early battle with them, but while scalps became trophies of war, they never achieved as much importance as counting coup.

None of this is to diminish the ferocity of battle between enemy tribes. Rivalries may have begun primarily to steal horses, but humans being what they are, escalation was inevitable. Even after the reservation era began, there were occasional opportunities for warriors to chase their old enemies. Plenty Coups, the Crow chief, was allowed by the government to pursue Blackfeet horse thieves from the Crow Reservation into the Bull Mountains north of Billings, Montana. When he caught up with his traditional enemies, he and his braves killed them by impaling them on sharpened stumps of lodgepole pine. Since Plenty Coups was considered extraordinarily kind by Indians and whites alike, many had trouble reconciling this action with the man they knew.

Failing to comprehend the depth and intensity of these rivalries prevents understanding the roles of various tribes during the warfare of the nineteenth

Chief Two Moon.

Chief Two Moon, Northern Cheyenne, 1906. When he was a little chief of the Kit Fox soldier society, Two Moon fought against Custer. One of the early prominent Cheyennes to realize that the tide of white settlers was overwhelming, Two Moon was a leader in negotiations with General Miles, helping to hold that officer to his early promise of a reservation for the Northern Cheyennes. Like American Horse, Two Moon was often sought as a representative of his tribe during the reservation era. It is said that his profile was one of three used for the composite image minted on the buffalo nickel.

century. For instance, there is much misunderstanding of the Crow and Shoshoni alliance with the white man against the Sioux and Cheyenne. People today often think the advancing white tide should have been the obvious enemy to anyone of Native American blood during that time, that all should have unquestioningly allied themselves against the whites. But tribal enmities did not suddenly dissolve. The Crow and Shoshoni did not lose their fear of the Sioux and Cheyenne, the tribes they considered primary threats to their territory and way of life, because the white man arrived on the scene. The Crows were coping with the white man fairly successfully on a political basis. The Sioux, on the other hand, were frequently raiding their reservation.

The army scout Luther S. Kelly encountered Two Moon (also Two Moons) in 1878 and gave us a word picture of the chief some thirty years younger than we see him in these photographs by Julia E. Tuell:

> . . . halfway between Fort Berthold and the mouth of the Yellowstone . . . I suddenly came upon a mounted Indian. I recognized him at once as Two Moons [sic], one of the chiefs who had fought us at Wolf Mountain the previous winter. We shook hands and proceeded on our way in perfect amity. . . . He was on his way back from the Middle West whither he had gone with other leading men to visit General Sheridan at his headquarters in Chicago on some mission . . . for the establishment of his people in or near the Yellowstone valley. A few months before we had been pursuing and fighting these Indians, who were about the wildest and fiercest on the plains. Now, in good fellowship, Two Moons and I rode along the trail, single file [which requires one to have his back to the other—DAA] as though we had always been the best of friends.
>
> Two Moons weighed about two hundred pounds and had a pleasant face. He wore a black felt hat with a feather and garnishing band, a woolen shirt, leggings, moccasins, and a painted robe adorned with picture writing. If he carried a revolver it was not in evidence. At the crossing of the Yellowstone he spied a wildcat high in a cottonwood tree and called my attention to it by pointing upward. I stopped and saw the animal on the topmost bough. I drew a bead on him and he fell almost at our feet, to the great satisfaction of my companion, who exclaimed, Ah-hii! Waste! or something to this effect, as though it was something of a feat. I skinned the beast and gave the pelt to him, which seemed to please him greatly.[3]

Kelly's estimate of two hundred pounds is easy to believe when we note the incredible depth of Two Moon's chest, visible in the profile photo, and the characterization fits as well—Two Moon was known as amiable, with a good sense of humor.

Movie footage taken in 1908 shows Two Moon describing the Custer battle in sign language. "The whole valley was filled with smoke," he said of that day on the Little Bighorn. "It took about as long as it takes for a hungry man to eat his dinner."

Scenes of Custer Battlefield (now Little Bighorn Battlefield) taken on the same day of the year (June 25th) in 1907, thirty-one years after the battle in which George Armstrong Custer and the contingent of the Seventh Cavalry with him died on a ridge above the river while Major Marcus Reno, and others of the command, were pinned on a hilltop about four miles away. Some two hundred sixty-five Seventh Cavalry soldiers died, while most estimate Indian losses as somewhat lower.

The wooden cross marked (in 1907) the spot where Custer fell. To the right in the foreground is the chipped marker for his brother Tom. The Custer brothers also lost a nephew in the battle. (The group of relatives was sometimes called derisively "The Royal Family" by the troops.) In the background is the valley of the Little Bighorn River where the Sioux and Cheyenne villages lay. The great victory was temporary. Opposition to the tribes hardened and an all-out military campaign returned most of the hostile bands to the reservations within a year.

Tribal enemies were admired, however, with the admiration only a warrior feels for another warrior whose bravery and skill he respects. Plenty Coups gave Linderman an unforgettable view of a magnificent force of Sioux warriors and of his respect for them when he described what in the West is called a "Mexican standoff" between the Sioux and the Crows. The Bighorn river was at flood

Early view of Custer Battlefield National Cemetery. Shortly after the battle, support began for a national cemetery on the battlefield. By the time Julia Tuell took this photo, dead from the Fetterman fight of 1866, the Hayfield fight of 1867 and the Bear Paw fight (with Chief Joseph) of 1877 had been relocated to the cemetery on the Little Bighorn. Two Moon, incidentally, was a young scout who evaluated enemy strength before the wiping out of Captain Fetterman and his men.

Close-up of the monument.

stage, too high to cross without becoming an easy target, and the Sioux were on the other side:

> . . . our Wolves [scouts] discovered the enemy in our country. He had already seen our village. There was no good to be gained by silence, or by trying to hide. But the Bighorn with its banks level-full was between us, and neither of us could cross it without giving the other a great advantage. So we showed off to each other and had a great time. I cannot tell you how beautiful the enemy looked, dressed in bright colors and wearing wonderful war-bonnets of eagle feathers that waved in the wind. Many rode pinto horses, and parties of young warriors would often dash toward the river as though they intended to swim it, giving their war-whoops and daring us to come over the water and fight them. As there was danger that they might attempt to cross, each time a band of Sioux rode to the river we raced down on our side to meet them, told them in signs what we thought of them, dared them to come over, and made great fun of them as warriors; but we had no thought of swimming the Bighorn in the face of such numbers. They were fine to look at, rushing in and out among the bushes that were loaded with reddening berries, the sunlight making their finery glisten; and out on the plains, where the wind played with the feathers on their bonnets, they were continually yelling and showing off as much for their own women as for us.[4]

The threat to the warrior way of life posed by masses of whites moving west did, of course, become the ultimate problem, but traditional enemies do not suddenly become friends in the face of a new threat any more on the plains of the Dakotas than they do in Bosnia. Rivalry between the tribes even exists today.

Some years ago I took a group of students to Pryor, Montana, to visit the Plenty Coups monument and museum and also the Little People caves, prominent in Crow mythology. We were guided by the mother of one of the students, a woman who was part Crow and who was married to a white rancher. After our Pryor visit we would proceed to Custer Battlefield (now the Little Bighorn Battlefield National Monument).

While waiting for the caretaker to open the museum, I chatted with our guide and a friend of hers, a Crow woman. The talk eventually led to two young men, juvenile delinquents according to the women, troublemakers. There was much shaking of heads as their latest ill deeds were recounted. Eventually the Crow woman looked at us and said, seriously and confidentially, "Well, they're half Cheyenne, you know." Both women nodded knowingly and went on to another topic. From their point of view this fact explained everything.

If the slashing tactics of Plains Indian warriors can be reflected in a game, basketball comes closest, the author feels. Especially in its boys' version, the game has assumed nearly religious importance on reservations today, but it has been played for quite some time by both sexes. Pictured is the 1928–1929 girls' team at Rosebud Boarding School, Mission, South Dakota, where Julia Tuell was matron. Nellie Star Boy, mentioned in chapter 1, is standing in the center with her friend Bertha Wooden Knife, a fine horsewoman, directly in front of her.

Here in Montana there is no greater sports confrontation than when one reservation basketball team takes on that of a rival. Indeed, the whole topic of basketball, which is now nearly a religion on Montana Indian reservations, is more germane to the business of Plains Indian warfare, and far less frivolous, than one might imagine. *Sports Illustrated* magazine recognized the cultural implications of the sport in its February 18, 1991, issue. In an article entitled "Shadow of a Nation" it honored an extraordinary Crow basketball player, Jonathan Takes Enemy, and dealt with the difficulty such talented athletes often have later in pursuing their basketball prowess at colleges off the reservation.

"Sioux Indian War Dance—Old men of the Rosebud Reservation of Sioux enjoying an early day war dance during a Fourth of July celebration. At this time their buckskin costumes, war paint, and feathers, beaded garments and every conceivable decoration are very much in vogue."—Julia Tuell.

Those who have never seen a reservation team cut loose in its "run and gun" offense with floor-length precision passes to players underneath the basket, drives through defenders or jump shots off 360-degree spins, have truly missed something even if they are not basketball fans. During my teaching years, coaches of my acquaintance often discussed the way to stop Indian teams. The consensus was that a team with disciplined defense stood the best chance, but that "letting them run," allowing even a crack of daylight, was like opening a fissure in the dam. The result would likely be a game out of control and a lopsided score.

Interestingly, the sports prowess so widespread on the basketball courts of reservation schools has not carried over, generally, to the football field. Although reservation schools in my own state occasionally field competitive football teams, there is clearly less love for the sport than there is for basketball. The reason is not lack of size among the Native American participants, for the Plains Indians are large people. This was also true a century ago. Because the U.S. Army tended to enlist smaller white men to be horse soldiers (smaller men tend to be better equestrians), it is said that the average Sioux or Cheyenne on the battlefield of the Little Bighorn was probably larger than his white counterpart. No, a close look at the nature of the two games reveals why the one so closely corresponds to cultural combat traditions while the other does not.

Football is a European war game. Each team has its own territory at its back, a territory marked by a border or frontier called the line of scrimmage. Players on defense struggle to defend this territory, to keep the "border" at its same location, or at least to give up as little territory as possible. To do this they tackle their enemy, sacrificing their bodies if need be. Players on offense throw themselves headlong at their enemy, blocking him to make a hole for a runner, who hurtles himself against the other team. If the offense is successful, the line of scrimmage moves and the team has gained territory.

Basketball, particularly the way it is played by reservation teams, is a blindingly quick game of hit and run, slash and pass. The Indian player feints, drives and counts coup on the basket. Territory is immaterial, and the Indian team often spends little time on defense. It will score, score and score, keeping its tally higher than the competition's. At its best the game is played with unmitigated joy. I have seen Indian ball players so thoroughly enjoy a humorous occurrence during a game that several baskets were scored on them before they got over their enjoyment of the joke.

Plains Indian warfare has been terribly misrepresented by Hollywood. The favorite cinematic shot of a thousand warriors, lined up on skyline, ready to charge into the path of murderous gunfire whenever the chief drops his lance, is a figment of the white imagination and is flawed on several points. Although Plains Indians did indulge in colorful displays of force, rarely did Indian warfare, at least in the West, occur with huge numbers of warriors. Most battles against other tribes were that of one village against another and probably involved fewer than a hundred warriors on each side and often forces much smaller. Ironically, one of the most publicized Plains Indian battles, the battle of the Little Bighorn, was so atypical as to be a historical aberration. That battle involved from 1,500 to 4,000 warriors (depending on whose estimates one accepts) pouring out from a series of villages stretching four miles along the creek bottom and containing, perhaps, as many as 15,000 Plains Indians. Though such numbers would have been modest in size compared to the great armies of Europe or to those of our American confrontation between North and South, they represented a mass of Indian warriors never seen before in the Northern Plains (and never to be seen again). Only a temporary alliance for survival formed by the remaining hostile tribes, a very brief coming together, could generate those relatively massive numbers.

Plains Indians, we must remember, lived off the land in movable villages. The logistics of supporting great numbers in a hunting economy made it impossible for large villages to sustain themselves very long. The Indian pony herd at the Little Bighorn numbered some 20,000, and it is said that little grass remained in a county-sized area when the Sioux and Cheyenne dispersed after their relatively short stay. An entire region was picked clean as a bone.

The battle of the Rosebud on the 17th of June, 1876 (about a week earlier than the Custer battle), although also outsized by Plains Indian standards, was more typical of the tactics warriors loved. On one side was a seasoned general named George Crook, his men totaling some 1,300, a thousand troopers of the Fifth Cavalry and other units supplemented by a band of Crows under Plenty Coups and another of Shoshonis under Tom Cosgrove. Cosgrove, a former cavalry captain, had drilled the Shoshonis in U.S. Cavalry maneuvers so successfully that they reported in with a flash of style and a demonstration of precision that left their white allies awed. On the other side were approximately 1,500 Sioux and Cheyenne warriors. The battlefield, in southeast Montana, was rolling foothills, perfect cavalry country.

The battle of the Rosebud lasted all day, and casualties on each side were relatively light, though slightly heavier among the Sioux and Cheyenne than among the men under Crook. The day was full of heroism on both sides, with charges, countercharges, courageous rescues of wounded comrades—and, unlike the situation after the battle of the Little Bighorn, plenty of survivors from both sides to tell the tale. Crook and his Crow and Shoshoni allies felt

Takes Them, old Sioux veteran warrior, in buffalo headdress, 1920.

Chief American Horse, Oglala Sioux. Like Two Moon and the Cheyenne American Horse, American Horse of the Sioux was a leader whose influence steadily increased throughout the reservation era. Like the Cheyenne chiefs mentioned, he was quick to see, after the wars of 1876 and 1877, that interaction with whites was inevitable, that advantageous negotiations were the best course of action. Known for his oratory, he took the position of leadership at the treaty conference of 1889 and was considered by many to be Red Cloud's successor as spokesman for the Oglalas. He then led the delegation of chiefs who traveled to Washington for a conference on the proposed agreement with President Harrison.

they had won and celebrated enthusiastically at their camp that evening. History gives the victory to Crazy Horse and the other leaders of the Sioux and Cheyenne, however, for by military standards mission is paramount. Crook's mission was to proceed north and link up with Terry, Custer and Gibbon. Instead, he had to turn south to Wyoming for resupply. The mission of Crook's enemies was to defend the huge concentration of Sioux and Cheyenne who were off the reservations and camped to their north, which they did successfully. Then they joined the massive village on the Little Bighorn, their confidence justly enhanced, and prepared for the arrival of Terry and Custer from the east. (The battlefield on the Rosebud, incidentally, has been bequeathed by the rancher who owned the land to be preserved as a historical park. It will not be developed like the Little Bighorn Battlefield, but will feature discreet markers highlighting this great meeting of Crook and Crazy Horse, the land being kept as natural as possible.)

But while the battle of the Rosebud would come closer to satisfying cinematic requirements than most, the Hollywood picture mentioned above is flawed in more than the numbers it depicts on each side. Plains Indians did not particularly like frontal assaults into enemy fire. It is true that warriors were taught death in battle was honorable and good, and their bravery was legion. The Cheyennes, in particular, often let their courage lead them to take terrible risks in battle, risks that took their toll in dead and wounded.

That said, the culture of the Plains Indians generally was one that did not like to take casualties. They did not accept scores of dead and wounded as an inevitable result of battle. A typical Indian band might number only a couple

---

During the Ghost Dance affair of the next two years, American Horse advocated moderation. At a standoff between Sioux policemen and participants in the Ghost Dance, when violence seemed imminent, a doctor named Eastman witnessed the commanding presence of American Horse, whose voice "rose above the din":

Stop! Think! What are you going to do? Kill these men of our own race? Then what? Kill all these helpless white men, women, and children? And what then? What will these brave words, brave deeds, lead to in the end? How long can you hold out? Your country is surrounded with a network of railroads; thousands of white soldiers will be here within three days. What ammunition have you? What provisions? Think, think my brothers! This is child's madness.[5]

American Horse was not successful, of course, in preventing the tragedy at Wounded Knee, but probably no one voice could have been. He died in 1908.

Runs Forward, Sioux, White River, South Dakota, 1913.

hundred people with perhaps thirty prime-of-life warriors. Each warrior was the fruit of a generation. There was no one to replace him when he was gone. No draft could be announced to conscript recruits. Since the tribes were rarely fighting to gain territory (they did not think in terms of land ownership defined by rigid borders), slashing guerrilla tactics suited their purposes far better than frontal assaults. Napoleon could go into battle with 300,000 men and accept the fact that winning the battle might cost one fourth of them. His way of fighting, of moving mass against mass, was consistent with his culture, and that culture accepted casualties as a fact of war.

The Hollywood picture also errs in its depiction of the chief as operating in the same manner as a white general. Whites on the frontier typically fancied Indians in their own image, and there is a tendency to do so still. One of the most difficult adjustments in white mentality of the time was overcoming the misconception that the signature of a single chief on a treaty was adequate, that it spoke for an entire tribe like the signature of a president, prime minister or king. Leadership among Plains tribes was complex. The Cheyenne tribe had two types of chief: council chiefs (of which there were forty-four) and chiefs or headmen of the warrior societies, who led fighting men into battle and were totally prepared to die doing so. Council chiefs were "peace chiefs," leaders of tribal government, welcome to fight, but as individuals. (I have never seen a Hollywood film that recognizes the difference.)

It is fair to consider the Plains Indian warrior as a soldier who retained a bit more individuality than his white counterpart. He was guided by social mores rather than by rigid military law. But his pursuit of war was not laissez-faire either, for there was a different set of rigid "rules" to be followed, a different but equally commanding authority over his head. That authority was spiritual. It was perfectly acceptable for a warrior or a chief, shortly before battle, to decide he would not participate, because it was not a good day to fight or to die. There was no disgrace in this, for the reason was not inconvenience or cowardice but spiritual necessity.

Plans for going to war were often accompanied by elaborate rituals, attempts to sense spiritual guidance. Grinnell tells how the Cheyennes used reflections in a badger's blood to predict the fate of warriors:

> . . . When men went afoot on the war-path [which they often did, intending to ride captured horses on the return trip], a badger was sometimes killed, the belly ripped open, all the entrails removed, but all the blood saved, and the animal left lying on its back on a bed of white sage on the ground with head toward the east till next morning, the blood remaining in the visceral cavity.

"Fording the Little White." Comes From Scout, here crossing the Little White River on the Rosebud Sioux Reservation in 1913, toured with Buffalo Bill's Wild West Show, traveling to England in the 1880s.

Next morning, the men who wished to do so unbraided the hair and, naked, walked by the badger, one after another, and each looked down at his reflection in the smooth surface of the blood. If in this mirror a man saw himself aged, wrinkled, and with white hair, he knew that he should live to be old; if he were soon to die the reflection would have its eyes closed. If the looker was to die of disease, he saw himself much emaciated. If he was to be killed and be scalped, the reflection appeared without scalp, and with bleeding head. It was like a looking glass. No man told another what he had seen. Usually the men who saw themselves scalped seemed downcast, turned back from the war-path, and returned to the village. The others went on. Not every member of the war-party looked into the blood; it was not obligatory.[6]

Comes From Scout family photograph, ca. 1913. Ben Scout, the future World War I soldier, stands in Sioux attire with feathers. George Scout is in Indian police uniform with star. Note elk-tooth dress on woman in center.

Spiritual evidence was usually honored utterly by Indian warriors, and on the few occasions they deviated from it, disaster seemed to fall. The great warrior Roman Nose (earliest of several Cheyennes who bore that name) died at Beecher's Island in a fight with Major George A. Forsyth. The sacred bonnet, a reproduction of that worn by Thunder himself and blessed by Thunder's power, was to have protected him, but failed. Roman Nose had earlier violated the ban on eating meat that had been touched by metal, a ban crucial to the bonnet's protective powers. Aware of his error in eating a stew stirred by a woman with a metal spoon, he first held back from the battle in which the Cheyennes had trapped Forsyth and his men on sandbar in Arikara Creek. When repeated charges failed to dislodge the enemy, Roman Nose let himself be goaded into battle by an old Dog Soldier who said he should be leading the young men into battle, not holding back. His pride led him into battle in spite of his knowledge of the inevitable outcome, and he died leading a charge, riddled by bullets.

Above and at left, Ben Scout, son of Comes From Scout , would continue the family's warrior tradition as a U.S. soldier and die in France during World War I. His body was returned for burial with honors.

Other warriors as well were sometimes inconvenienced, even exasperated, by the limitations imposed by spiritual concerns. War parties could not leave a Cheyenne camp if the Mahuts (Maahotse), the Sacred Arrows, were stained with blood and needed renewal, not a common situation but one involving considerable ceremony on those occasions renewal was required. During Sun Dances, held around the time of the summer equinox, the entire tribe had to be present in camp. But Grinnell discusses two Cheyenne leaders, Yellow Wolf and Elk River, both extremely accomplished at taking horses, who dispensed with many of the normally required ceremonies:

> On the occasion in 1828 when Yellow Wolf took a great band of horses from the Comanches under Bull Hump, he told his young men that he did not wish to have the usual customs as to the leader observed with him on this trip. Neither would he carry the pipe.
> "These ceremonies," he said, "oblige us to avoid too many things. If we should fail to observe some law or some custom we might be obliged to turn back. On this trip [referring to the rule that leaders were not to ask for food or drink but that it was to be offered to them] I will get my own water and cook my own food, and in these matters will be just like any of you. But I wish you to remember that I am still the head of this party."[7]

When a warrior's medicine (spiritual power) was extremely strong he had a confidence that bred fearlessness. He might rush into battle crying, "It is a good day to die!" as many did on that Sunday in June 1876, when the Sioux and Cheyenne overwhelmed Custer. Earlier, the Sioux chief Sitting Bull had undertaken a Sun Dance, had directed fifty small pieces of flesh to be cut from each of his arms. He had then dreamed of white soldiers plummeting headfirst, their hats falling off, directly into the Sioux camp. The vision was taken to mean that the soldiers would come and be destroyed by the Sioux and Cheyenne.

Spiritual motivation (in this case partially inspired by Christianity) also lay behind the last great movement of the Sioux to resist white authority. The Ghost Dance religion, the belief that a Messiah would come and restore the "Great Circle" of Plains Indian life, fueled the terrible events that led to the massacre at Wounded Knee. This last fight between white and Sioux happened only a short distance west of the Sioux schools tended by P.V. and Julia Tuell a couple of decades later.

In addition to this powerful spiritual dimension of the warrior's psyche there was another motivation, perhaps easier for white culture to understand, that of membership in soldier or warrior societies. Even today, large military units

Black Bull, Sioux, 1916.

John Fast Horse, Sioux, 1913. Note hair trim on war shirt, possibly from scalp locks taken during war years.

John Thunder Elk (nicknamed "Sore Eyes"). As a little boy, Varble called him by his nickname and Thunder Elk expressed his displeasure by holding up his hands to indicate elk horns and saying, "Me John Thunder Elk." 1920.

encourage *esprit de corps*, and it's understood that small, exclusive units are conducive to fighting camaraderie. Thus, the current U.S. Army has its Green Berets and its 101st Airborne. Plains Indian soldier societies, such as the Kit Foxes, Crazy Dogs and Red Shields among the Cheyenne were military forces for warfare and policemen for more domestic requirements. Membership often even crossed tribal lines, some societies counting members among both the Sioux and Cheyenne, for instance, and the practice has persisted. Warrior societies survived the reservation era and exist today among the Cheyenne.

Members of a given society used their own unique war paint and had exclusive ceremonies and dances. Often they carried distinctive pieces of equipment. Grinnell tells us that the bravest men of the Elk-Horn Scrapers carried "two crooked lances—shaped at one end like a shepherd's crook—and two straight lances. . . . The shafts of these lances were wrapped with strips of otter skin, and at four different points along the shaft of each, two eagle feathers were tied."[8]

Red Fish, Sioux, was a veteran of the early battles. 1916.

Caught-The-Eagle, Sioux.

Grinnell also tells of a fascinating feminine side to war societies of the Cheyenne:

> To each soldier band belonged four young women, usually girls—though some might be married—of a good family. They joined in the dance, and sometimes sat by the singers and sang with them. If the soldiers made a dance, or went from one place to another, feasting, the women were with them, but if the camp was moving the girls traveled with their families. Their duties were chiefly social; that is to say, they were present at meetings of the band, took part in singing and dancing, and sometimes cooked for the soldiers. They were not necessarily related to anyone in the band, but were supposed to be girls of the best families in the camp. If one of them resigned . . . another was selected to fill her place by the soldier chiefs. When a girl had been chosen, two young men were sent to her lodge to bring her. The position was an honorable one.
>
> Such a girl was spoken of as *nut uhk e a,* female soldier. Usually a good-looking girl was chosen, who devoted herself to the position in much the same spirit that a nun gives herself up to her vocation. The girl was not compelled to retain this position; if she wished to marry, she might resign, and often did so.[9]

The warrior tradition was all-important among Plains Indian males, and even our cursory examination of it suggests its complexity. The exact state of warrior mentality when Julia Tuell photographed among the Sioux and Cheyenne is difficult to determine. The necessity (or opportunity) to make war with neighbors of other tribes was gone. War with the white man also no longer existed nor was contemplated. Until World War I (when so many Native Americans enlisted and fought on the battlefields of Europe) the fever to fight for the United States at large had not engaged the Cheyenne and Sioux fighting spirit.

But even in those dark days of the early reservation era there was pride in having been a fighting man of the Sioux and Cheyenne. The warrior societies were intact. Julia Tuell had a never-to-be repeated opportunity, and she made the most of it. Two Moon, both chiefs named American Horse, Black Bull, Comes From Scout, Runs Forward, Takes Them—these were the last of the real ones, veterans who had taken horses from their enemies, withstood his fire and protected their villages with integrity and ferocity. Julia came to know them. They posed for her camera and talked freely with her. On the faces she has given us are indelibly stamped courage and character and memories of things that will never be seen again.

THE OTHER LIFE

BEFORE A YOUNG MAN BECAME A WARRIOR, before he courted and married, before he ventured to call himself a man, he went on a quest that would take him to the very edge physically, psychologically and spiritually. Whether Sioux, Cheyenne, Crow, Assiniboin or Blackfeet, he did this, for this quest transcended tribal division, put him in common with other young men from other tribes, even those of his enemies, who did likewise.

When the time seemed right the boy was taken by his mentor to a hill or butte or mountain, a place known for its spiritual power, a place where he could watch the topsides of eagles' wings below him. If Cheyenne, the boy was under the direction of a priest who had himself undergone the vision quest, then had been empowered spiritually to instruct others. Refusing to eat or drink, sweating under the blazing sun and at night shivering when it dropped behind the horizon and the canyon wind blew, the boy waited. Sometimes he had to lie motionless for hours. If Sioux, his waiting was in a vision pit dug into the hilltop.

Days passed. His throat grew tight with thirst, and the pang of his empty stomach grew to a dull throb. The sun burned. Sometimes it seemed he was not alone, that he heard voices, voices which he answered. And then, if he was lucky, he got what he sought: a vision. Often this happened on the fourth and last day. His dream might be very complex but so vivid he would remember every detail to tell the holy men back at the village later. Sometimes it was simple. What the vision told him was crucial, for if all went well he would come down from the mountain with a new, more profound view of himself. He would then know his "medicine," a poor English translation of native words that mean something more like "spiritual power." His vision quest was a search for spiritual self-knowledge, a quest to learn where his spiritual power lay. With this power he could also have physical power. He could be a great warrior and leader. Without it, he was severely limited.

Northern Cheyenne sweat lodge, 1907. Universally present among Northern Plains Indian tribes, the sweat lodge was used for both spiritual and medicinal purposes. Here, rocks are being heated in the fire.

Thomas E. Mails described the vision quest as follows:

. . . it is the custom to seek, or to go in search of, a vision. Black Elk taught that visions take the viewer to literal places where things are and exist. The seeker must then find that place.

The belief is that a person cannot be a success in any aspect of life without the Great Spirit's help. The way to obtain this assistance is through supernatural helpers whom God has created and empowered for this very purpose. The first contact with these helpers is made in a vision, and it is continued in dreams, subsequent visions, and as encounters take place with earthly counterparts of the visioned helper.

In preparation for the sweat bath, rocks will be removed from the fire with a pitchfork, a modern (1907) innovation: Formerly a forked stick would have been used. The hot rocks will be placed in a shallow depression in the sweat lodge. Water poured over them will produce a dense steam.

For instance, one might experience in his vision a giant wolf. Shortly thereafter, the seeker obtains some part of the wolf to be carried in his medicine bundle as a constant reminder of the experience; and from that moment on the wolf is in his consciousness in every prayer and ceremony. Moreover, when a real wolf appears as the man journeys, he holds a conversation with it in the absolute belief that it is his spiritual helper.[1]

Sometimes no vision came. When that happened the young man returned to the village sadly, but resolved to try again. In a few cases no vision quest succeeded even after repeated attempts, so that the young man, like Two-Leggings

Northern Cheyenne Medicine Man about to enter sweat lodge. Most religious ceremonies were preceded by sweat baths. Before a hunt or a military campaign, holy men would sometimes enter the sweat bath with participants and consecrate a particular weapon or article of clothing, helping to insure success.

of the Crows, went through life with a sort of disability. Two-Leggings was pitied for his inability to dream and was actually given medicine by another warrior who had been amply blessed.

The cynic may wonder why a boy unable to dream would not simply make up a story to impress the village, to give him the medicine he needed. But the explanation of honesty in these matters is quite simple: belief, faith. Only a true vision could give one power, so charades were out of the question.

The vision (or dream) sometimes was painted in broad, prophetic strokes, giving the warrior-to-be a peek at the future. The Lakota mystic Black Elk, at age nine, had a vision so complex as to formulate an entire theology. It occurred during a time when his family thought he was desperately ill, before the age he would have formally sought it. His life was forever changed, forever dedicated to restoring the "Great Circle" of Sioux life, the old economy, spirituality and

"An Evening's Smoke." The pipe was a sacred ingredient of all holy ceremonies as well as the taking of oaths or the setting up of treaties.

Northern Cheyennes gathered for a celebration near Busby, Montana, in 1907.

mode of living the Sioux saw symbolized in the circle and which they had lost with the reservation era.

More commonly the vision revealed a bird or animal or object that contained the young man's spiritual power. Depending on his tribe, his name might now be altered, and the thing that was now his medicine was always with him thereafter, symbolically or physically.

Approaches to the vision quest varied considerably. Sometimes self-torture (beyond subjecting oneself to solitude, hunger, thirst, cold and heat) was involved. The Cheyennes said, for instance, that piercing of the flesh was not originally part of the Sun Dance, that it was incorporated into that sacred ceremony from individual vision quests, a sort of merger between the two. They made this point as part of their case for resumption of the Sun Dance after

"Northern Cheyenne Medicine Man at Work." The terms "medicine man" or "medicine woman" are often used generically to indicate both healers and holy men or priests, but the two roles were in fact separate, although some individuals were both. Regarding the Sioux, Thomas E. Mails states, "A medicine man is a doctor who practices healing. He is not necessarily a priest as well. If he is both, then he is more properly called a holy man. Thus, a holy man is a prophet and spiritual counselor in addition to being a healer."[2]

reservation officials had banned it. The Lakota (Sioux) holy man John (Fire) Lame Deer had with him on his vision quest a gourd containing forty small pieces of flesh his grandmother had cut from her arm. But always the four days of the vision quest combined prayer, fasting and sacrifice in some form.

It seems to me that of all the coming-of-age rituals found in various cultures and religions, none is more singularly spiritual than the vision quest. Some of these rituals have a social component as well, its level of importance depending on where the event is practiced. But the vision quest contains not only considerable

"Red Cherries, a good type of the earlier day Medicine Man . . . one of fame among his tribesmen, the Northern Cheyennes. He had numerous calls to most every part of the reservation, and with the intense shaking of his medicine rattle . . . his mode of administering to the sick made the nights weird and most primitive."—Julia Tuell.

Northern Cheyenne medicine man's home and family, 1906. The holy man's sacred bundle is tied to the pole behind and to right of tent.

sacrificial suffering, it involves total immersion into a spiritual world utterly real to the pledger, and a blueprint, unique to him, for the rest of his life.

The world of the Plains Indian was intensely spiritual. The theology of the Sioux and Cheyenne was complex, as were their rituals and ceremonies for practicing their religion. It goes far beyond the scope of this book (and of this author) to attempt proper descriptions of the Sun Dance (also called The Medicine Lodge by the Cheyenne) and the Massaum. Without many years of study one does not venture to capture the theology of a culture on the printed page. It is far better to refer the reader who is searching for enlightenment to those who have spent their lives in the scholarship necessary, people such as George Bird Grinnell, oft-quoted in this book, a great scholar who was not always given complete information in those early days when he worked with the Cheyennes;

Cheyenne camp showing the willow frames of sweat lodges, center and right.

Father Peter J. Powell, whose *Sweet Medicine* was a thoroughly enjoyable revelation to me; and anthropologist Karl H. Schlesier, whose *Wolves of Heaven* traces the Massaum from its earliest origins, disputing along the way many previously held assumptions.

When the reservation era began, many of the Sioux and Cheyenne sacred ceremonies were banned by the U.S. government. Very few whites at the time had anything like a scholarly knowledge of the meaning of such ceremonies in the cultures involved, and even if they had, their voices in that era may not have carried much weight. In an advancing white civilization, which tended to consider religions outside the Judeo-Christian tradition to be heathen or barbaric, there was little sympathy for the religions of other cultures. Also, few people understood that many of the ceremonies represented religion at all.

A medicine man named Mexican Cheyenne near Lame Deer, 1907. Varble Tuell, many years later, met Mexican Cheyenne's grandson who produced with delight the deertail necklace worn in the photograph. (The grandson had never seen a photograph of Mexican Cheyenne.)

Lakota woman with dog travois, on her way to a dog feast celebration in the Oak Creek district of the Rosebud Sioux Reservation, ca. 1918.

Dog feast celebration, Rosebud Reservation. Julia Tuell's Model T is in background to right.

Further, the purpose and meaning of the ceremonies was simply misunderstood. The Sun Dance was thought by most whites (many still have this misconception) to be primarily a test of bravery and endurance for an individual warrior. Whites focused on the self-torture, the slitting of the warrior's breasts or back and the hanging or pulling against skewers inserted through these slits, as the central event of the ceremony. Few probably knew that the torture was a sacrifice, that the ceremony was not just the proving of one individual's mettle but the symbolic renewing of the spiritual well-being of an entire people. The very few who knew of the parallel sacrifice of Sacred Woman in the Cheyenne version (touched upon in chapter 2) misinterpreted it with equal vehemence.

Nor had it escaped the notice of whites that Sun Dances had preceded major episodes of Indian hostility. We have mentioned Sitting Bull's Sun Dance held shortly before the battle of the Little Bighorn. Again, the reasons were misunderstood, the erroneous conclusion being that the Sun Dance was a sort of lethal

Sioux celebration, 1920. Note shell capes worn by women.

pep rally. The influence of early reservation missionaries was also a factor, as were the changed attitudes of tribal members who had been converted to Christianity and now questioned the rightness of the ceremonies. (Christianity influenced the Plains Indians from the early 1800s, with many denominations represented when the reservations developed. Many Native Americans today are devout Christians.)

By 1897 the Sun Dance had been outlawed on the Northern Cheyenne Reservation. On the Rosebud and Pine Ridge Sioux reservations a similar pattern transpired, first with orders from the Indian agents to cease holding the dances on their respective reservations. Finally, in 1904, a law issued by the Interior Department outlawed the Sun Dance on a federal level.

Sioux men dressed for war dance near White River, South Dakota, on the Rosebud Reservation, ca. 1920.

The effects on the Sioux and Cheyenne were devastating. This was the outlawing of the right to practice their religion, key to which were the Sun Dance and other ceremonies of spiritual renewal. One would expect this prohibition to force the religion underground, to force performance of it in secret as has happened so many times in world history when a dominant culture has refused to allow a minority to worship as it pleased. To a degree this did occur, the ceremonies being modified to make them easier to hide from non-Indian eyes. But holding a Sun Dance secretly was a difficult proposition. To be fully and properly executed, the event required days to prepare and several more to perform, and it involved building structures and gathering together virtually everyone in the tribe.

Thus, following passage of the laws against the Sun Dance, a ceaseless struggle to lift the ban began. It succeeded, finally, in 1934 with the Indian Reorganization Act. That federal law guaranteed free religious expression to

The Sun Dance (called by the Cheyennes "The New Life Lodge"), is the great sacred world-renewing ceremony of both the Cheyenne and Lakota peoples. For a time it was banned on the Northern Cheyenne Reservation by white reservation officials who misunderstood its purpose and particularly objected to the public sacrifice of the pledger's flesh. This sacrifice was practiced in versions of the Sun Dance common to most Northern Plains tribes and was considered by whites to be self-mutilation. Depending on the tribe, the sacrifice of the flesh involved perforation of the pledger's breasts or back and his hanging by skewers from the Sun Pole (or his pulling against it until the flesh gave way). In a private communication to the author, Father Peter J. Powell says that today, however, "The New Life Lodge flourishes as the great central act of Northern Cheyenne worship."

Julia E. Tuell photographed this offering of the Sun Dance in 1911, the same summer George Bird Grinnell recorded the Sun Dance and Massaum ceremonies.

Here the great center pole is being painted by the pledger under the guidance of the instructor priest.

The Sun Dance altar.

Cheyenne participants in the Sun Dance.

The altar in the Cheyenne Sun Dance lodge.

Appears to show preparation for tying pledger to Sun Pole. In the modified version, a man was hung from ropes under his arms rather than through his flesh (Lakota).

Native Americans. But before that, as Father Peter J. Powell delineates, the Cheyennes worked hard to persuade the white man to allow practice of the Sun Dance, becoming more effective tactically as they came to know the government better. In 1907 a group of chiefs and headmen, Two Moon, American Horse, Crazy Head, Brave Bear and Little Sun (Two Moon and American Horse are pictured in this book), worked diplomatically with Superintendent J.C. Eddy at Lame Deer. Making the case that the torture was a relatively recent addition to the Sun Dance and that it was unnecessary, these men persuaded Eddy that the dance was a positive religious experience for all and that it should be allowed under the name "Willow Dance." The leaders pointed out that the Sun Dance was meaningful for people of all races and for Christians. (Few who know it well dispute this point.) Thus, the Sun Dance, under its new name and without the pledger hanging from the center pole, was held yearly until 1911, when Washington firmly banned its celebration and that of all similar ceremonies. The reason given for the new ban was that the celebration took the Cheyennes away too long from work on their ranches.[3]

Sometimes history contains happy coincidences, and the fact that a temporary renewal of the Sun Dance and Massaum occurred at this particular point, from 1907 until 1911, is one of those, for Julia Tuell and her camera were at Lame Deer during this time. Her photographs of the Massaum, a ceremony today extinct, were most likely of the 1911 occasion and are among the very few that exist. According to Karl H. Schlesier these were the last performances of the Massaum among the Northern Cheyennes, with only one full-fledged performance being held later, in 1927, by the Southern Cheyennes.[4]

During the early part of the twentieth century when major Indian ceremonies *were* allowed, they were often scheduled for the Fourth of July celebration. It was customary for whites to take several days off work during this holiday, and since the Sun Dance and other ceremonies required four days or more for

Above and at right, Lakota Sun Dance ceremony, ca. 1920.

The Lakota holy man Black Elk said, "Everything the Power of the World does is done in a circle." The photograph shows Sioux at the Rosebud Reservation assembled for a ceremony.

proper observance, the tribes saw the combination as logical. Further, they knew white reservation officials would be more cooperative in allowing the Sun Dance during a holiday, and since the ceremony had once been corresponded with the summer equinox, Independence Day was close to the traditional time. This combination of events and the sense of national patriotism growing rapidly among the Sioux and Cheyenne in those years leading up to World War I explain the American flags flying from the tepees seen in many photographs of such events. As time passed, flying the flag of the United States became common no matter when celebrations were scheduled.

The most sacred geometric shape to the Plains Indians was the circle. "Everything the Power of the World does is done in a circle," said Black Elk, the Sioux holy man. The heavenly bodies are circles, as is the life of a man. The seasons move through a circle. Early reservation Indians forced to live in square log cabins suffered, they felt, from being deprived of the power of circular dwellings. The white man's railroad and telegraph ran in odd straight lines. As we've mentioned, Plains Indians often referred to the cessation of their free-roaming life as the breaking of the Great Circle.

Thus it is no surprise that the Sioux perform the Sun Dance in a large circle. At its center the participants erect a trimmed and painted tree called the sacred tree or sun pole. The main entrance to the circle is to the east, just as Plains Indian villages were normally built (in circles with lodges facing east and an entrance to the east). Close by are one or more sweat lodges to provide purification for the participants, a key element in many ceremonial activities, and a lodge for preparation, dressing and painting.[5]

Below and on following page, scenes ca. 1920 on Rosebud Sioux Reservation during the years the full Sun Dance could not be legally (publicly) performed. The Sacred Tree is in evidence in the center of the circle, suggestive of some version of the Sun Dance.

Here again we must generalize, for there were many differences between the Sun Dance as performed in various tribes and also between its performance in pre-reservation times and today. (We can say "today" and speak of the Sun Dance in the present tense, for versions of it are now being widely celebrated on Northern Plains Indian reservations.) But all versions seem to share certain elements: the circle, the sacred tree and a pledger (sometimes several) who undergoes the sacrifice. Terminology for each of these varies. There may be a sacred woman (often the wife of the pledger) who sacrifices also in the Cheyenne version, and there is an instructor, who appears to be the primary figure of spiritual authority. Further spiritual support and instruction are drawn from priests and additional instructors. The picture is not one of a single individual who goes through trials alone, but the more gratifying one of a pledger supported step by step, encouraged not only by the staff most involved in the dance but by the entire tribe. His health and success are theirs as well, and his (or her) triumph will belong to all.

Normally practiced today for four days (plus preparation time), the Sun Dance moves through an elaborate sequence that involves prayer, dance and sacrifice. Virtually all elements of the tribe's spirituality are touched upon in some way. The effect is a profound renewal of spiritual well-being not only for the tribe, but in Cheyenne and Lakota belief, for all creation. All is renewed by the sacred power flowing from the Sun Dance Lodge.

We are fortunate in having several detailed accounts of Sun Dances past and present written by scholars who have witnessed the ceremonies. These studies (by authors I have cited frequently in this book) are for the reader interested in more than this brief sketch. George Bird Grinnell in *The Cheyenne Indians* devotes the chapter "Medicine Lodge" (Vol. II, pp. 211–284) to the 1911 Sun Dance held near Lame Deer. This account is of particular interest, because the ceremony described is the one photographed by Julia Tuell and pictured here.

Father Peter J. Powell devotes much of the second volume of *Sweet Medicine* to describing with both text and photographs a Sun Dance fifty years later, in 1961, again held by the Northern Cheyennes at Lame Deer (but it is important to read *both* volumes for the continuity of Cheyenne spirituality provided). Although Father Powell centers on the 1961 ceremony, he witnessed Sun Dances held by the Northern Cheyennes in 1959, 1962 and 1964 as well, and attended the Southern Cheyenne Sun Dance in 1960 in Oklahoma. A trusted friend and adopted member of the tribe, Father Powell has assisted since then in the ceremony of bringing Esevone, the Sacred Buffalo Hat, into the camp, part of the ritual. (Father Powell is also the first white man to

The Massaum or Animal Dance, an elusive, earth-giving ceremony of the Cheyenne tribe, was performed for the last time in 1927 among the Southern Cheyennes. This 1911 ceremony, photographed by Julia E. Tuell and described in detail by George Bird Grinnell in *The Cheyenne Indians*, was the last performed by the Northern Cheyennes.

have participated in the traditional four days' fasting on the Cheyenne Sacred Mountain.)

Sundancing at Rosebud and Pine Ridge by Thomas E. Mails and other contributors concentrates on the Oglala and Brulé Sioux (both Teton Lakota) who live on the two Sioux reservations, and focuses on the background of the Sun Dance and its present-day expression. There are many photographs in a detailed sequence of a Sun Dance, complete with the flesh-piercing procedure, held in 1974 by the Sioux. Mails is a gifted artist, and his oil paintings enhance the text. Again there is a connection with Julia Tuell, for there is reference to Sun Dance ceremonies held during the years she was at the Rosebud Reservation and which she photographed.

The Massaum ceremony is distinctly Cheyenne (though Karl H. Schlesier has traced its roots to Siberia and the subarctic, to peoples with related beliefs). The ceremony is elusive and involved. As mentioned above, the Northern Cheyenne Massaum celebrations in 1909 and 1911 were two of the last three performed. Grinnell described the 1911 event, while the Julia Tuell photographs, some of

At left and above, scenes from the Contrary Dance within the Massaum. Contraries were people who acted in opposites, doing the reverse of what was considered normal. Although their roles as tribal members were partly comic, Grinnell says they were braves of considerable importance "and were often trusted with serious duties—even with leadership—in battle."[6] In the Massaum ceremony, the contraries, "white-painted except as to necks and upper shoulders . . . represented hunters . . . They carried red-painted bows and arrows which they held and used in a reversed way . . . They acted in an eccentric way, and darted hither and thither unexpectedly."[7]

Karl H. Schlesier further describes the role of the contraries in the Massaum:

From the Hohnuhka lodge seven contraries (Thunder Spirits) ran up, dressed only in breechclout, with their body and hair painted white. The hair that was tied in a knot over the forehead was decorated with a single eagle feather. They carried miniature sky lances painted red. [In early times—DAA] After the bow and arrow had been adopted, they used miniature sky bows and four types of miniature arrows. Here they acted as sacred hunters, emhoniu, and because they were ritually in a contrary condition as sacred cows. They passed along the sacred animals milling around in the pound, ritually killing with stabbing motions. Animals who were struck staggered and fell, spurting blood, but raised themselves again. The mimicry in the display of injured and bleeding animals was extraordinary.[8]

Schlesier goes on to describe the healing process that follows the contraries, in which the animals ritualistically healed any sick or injured members of the tribe, who sat motionless in front of their lodges, waiting for the animal blessing.

A black buffalo dancer in the Massaum.

which he used in *The Cheyenne Indians*, appear to date from that same observance. The Massaum (also called the Animal Dance) has been called an earth-giving or earth-renewing ceremony. It did have certain elements in common with the Sun Dance. A Sacred Tree was selected and cut with great ceremony, then set into a hole in the center of the circle. As in the Sun Dance there were pledgers and instructors, usually a male and female of each, often man and wife. A square lodge was erected on four poles around the Sacred Tree, which protruded from the top. Each of the four poles around the Sacred Tree marked one of the sacred directions, and since the four poles ring the center tree, the effect is circular, even though the structure is square. What followed erection of the structure was an extraordinarily complex five-day ceremony. Initially the

Julia E. Tuell's note: "Tribe offering unto the wolf hide on the scaffold, headman in act of praying unto same, Wolf Dance, Massaum Ceremony."

Wolf Dance—"[yellow] wolf hide adorned with offering, Massaum Ceremony."—Julia Tuell.

universe, the earth and creation were symbolically established with the male instructor acting as Maheo, the supreme being.

Of great importance to the ceremony was the sacred buffalo skull. The first photograph on page 162 shows the buffalo skull being carried to its position in the shade prior to being painted. (This is a detail from the Tuell photograph used in Grinnell's *The Cheyenne Indians*.) Julia Tuell's notes are of interest: "The Medicine Buffalo Skull, used in all the tribal ceremonies of the Northern Cheyennes . . . was held in great reverence among them. In this scene it was decorated for a rare ceremony [the Massaum] in 1911, the first time they had held such ceremony for twenty years before that date, or since 1891." Note the sunken arrangement of the "altar" for the skull. The beginning of the ceremonies took place under cover of their lodge; the white man was not permitted to see the rites. The second and third photographs, on pages 162 and 163, show the sacred buffalo skull painted for the Massaum ceremony.

Yellow Wolf entering and leaving the Wolf Lodge. A yellow and a gray wolf (sometimes described as a white and red wolf) were important in the Massaum. Movements of both during the ceremony were complex and included circling the camp (a circle of approximately two miles, according to Julia Tuell's notes), part of making the camp into the universe, holy within and without.

"Massaum Ceremony, where
medicine man has borne buffalo
skull into other lodge and all are
seated about in a circle."
—Julia Tuell.

Sioux encampment, July Fourth celebration. Note American flags on door pins, front of tepee. During early reservation days, Native American celebrations were often scheduled to coincide with the holiday on Independence Day.

Karl H. Schlesier describes the significance of the markings on the skull:

> The woman pledger left the lodge and returned carrying a buffalo skull, placing it on the west side of the sage-covered bench facing the world tree. The skull was painted by the male instructor after the eye sockets and the nasal cavity had been filled with round bundles of grass. The male instructor drew a black line from the back of the skull down its center to the nasal opening, then traced along both sides of the black line, two lines with white color. The remainder of the skull, including the horn cores, was covered with dry red paint. The three lines represented day and night; the red paint of the skull the earth. Next the three grass plugs were painted red; they represented all the vegetation that grows from the earth.
>
> On the top of the skull, between the horn cores and the eyes, a drawing in solid blue was executed, resembling in form a German iron cross; this represented the blue star of midsummer dawn (Rigel). When a solid red disk (the sun) was painted on her right jaw and a black crescent (the moon) on the left, Esceheman [Our Grandmother Earth] had been made and was ritually present.[9]

As the days pass both male and female Instructors and other participants assume the symbolic roles of portions of the universe and of earth. Key were the five major spirits, the two wolves and the kit fox. The dance employs mimic performances of many members of the animal kingdom, contraries (people who act opposite of normal) and a sacred, ritual hunt. To a layman such as myself, the ceremony appears to progress flowingly, like the movements of a symphony or the unfolding of a five-act drama. The impression left is that of renewal, a sense of the rightness of things, the epitome of "God's in his heaven and all's right with the world." Harmony throughout all deities in the heavens and creatures on earth seems to be conveyed, man's place within the animal kingdom secure and respectful of all other members.

And this, after all, was the Plains Indians' ideal. This was the balance that was shattered when these small tribes were overwhelmed by a powerful civilization. This other world, this spiritual world, was the place occupied much of the time by each woman and warrior. Every piece of their environment had a spiritual dimension.

Often in this book I have pointed out that Julia Tuell and her camera were at the right places at the right times, that she captured things which floated by as if in a swift creek, soon to disappear forever. There is a temptation to place her fortunate presence during the observance of complicated religious rituals— particularly at Lame Deer in the first part of this century—into this category as well. Then we remember that so often through cataclysmic human events, it is the spiritual side of mankind that survives. The Sun Dance is again being practiced. The other world of Plains Indian existence is still a reality.

Postlude

In the late 1970s, while teaching in the small town of Bridger, Montana, I first met Varble Tuell. A custodian at our high school, Varble was in his youthful sixties, congenial, anxious to tell of the many places he had lived and his many interesting experiences before settling into this "retirement" job. I'd been told he had much artistic talent.

I was offering at that time an elective course in Montana history, one in which I concentrated on the history of the Yellowstone Basin. Our primary text was Mark Brown's *The Plainsmen of the Yellowstone,* which we supplemented with Linderman's *Plenty Coups: Chief of the Crows,* Luther S. Kelly's *Yellowstone Kelly,* Dorothy Johnson's *The Bloody Bozeman* and several more. Geographically, we could not have been in a more perfect place to immerse ourselves in a fascinating past. Out the schoolhouse door to the east, close enough that I could see the individual trees within the mountain blue, were the Pryor Mountains, named after the sergeant who accompanied Lewis and Clark. The Clark's Fork of the Yellowstone ran through our town (named for the Clark of that same expedition), and the town itself was named after Bridger's Crossing. The trails scouted out in the 1860s by both Jim Bridger and his rival John Bozeman forded the river close to town. Chief Joseph cannily led his band of Nez Percé right over the ground where our high school stood, after throwing the army a curve farther south. (Warriors dragged small trees from their saddles to create a dust down into Wyoming while the bulk of the tribe headed north.) And later, once our town had come to be, Calamity Jane had been, for a while, a resident.

In an hour I could drive my old GMC pickup (or guide the school bus driver on field trips—I did both) over a gravel road heading east, turn north on a county road that was once the grade of a narrow-gauge railroad built by Chinese workers under Mormon contractors, and hit that historic passageway between mountains, traveled by explorer Laroque (and almost everyone else important in Montana history), Pryor Gap. In it was a long railroad tunnel through which we hiked, its chiseled sides cool and damp. (I understand that it has now fallen in.)

In another half hour north we could be in Pryor, Montana, site of Plenty Coups' home and museum, just past the ranch that contains the Little People

Woostah (Vo'estaa'e) gives the Tuell girls lessons in the bow and arrow.

caves (to the west), and Castle Rock (to the east), a favorite vision quest site for the Crows. Then, east, on a good paved (but little-used) highway, an hour or so away was Custer Battlefield (now Little Bighorn Battlefield). It was fine on a spring day to go to these places with a bunch of jabbering high-school kids, when the musty halls of the school cried "escape, escape," and the meadowlarks sang in the sage.

It was, I think, in 1978 that Varble mentioned his mother had taken wonderful photographs of some of the people we studied in the Montana history class. I had vaguely been aware of her photography from earlier conversations, but I was busy, and I suspect I had not listened well. Would I, Varble wanted to know, like him to bring up some of his mother's framed photographs and make up a display in my classroom for the students? Absolutely, I told him. Never having been a teacher who cared to spend much time on classroom decorations or on that darling of school administrators, the bulletin board, I was only too happy to have someone shoulder part of the load and spruce things up.

But I was stunned when I walked into my classroom the next morning. Ringing the room in rustic wooden frames of his own making was Varble's treasure. Two chiefs named American Horse, Two Moon, Dull Knife's daughter, the Madonna of the Rosebud—they looked upon my nondescript room with quiet dignity and transformed the place into a shrine. And there was more, photograph albums impeccably arranged with many more images in black and white and in Julia's colored hand tinting. On the blackboard, in colored chalk, was a mural sketched by Varble of the battlefield of the Little Bighorn.

I suppose this book began on that day, although we did not know it. Just when Varble and I began our refrain, "Someday we'll have to put a book together . . . , " I can't exactly recall. But I know it lasted through a hectic double life during the years I taught full time and ranched full time at locations sixty miles apart and tried to become a published author while I was at it. I know our discussion lasted through Varble's second retirement and my first publication of outdoor and horse-magazine articles, then of my first two books. I know it recurred every time we met, and I know Varble was patient, realizing that the time for me had to be right. And I was patient too, when he seemed anxious to do the project but hesitant, as I was, to take the first concrete steps.

Well, we got over it. Most of Julia's photographs have been hidden all too long. It is time they spoke to more people, and we hope they will do so now.

We began this book with an invocation stimulated by the photo of Chief American Horse of the Northern Cheyennes holding Julia Tuell's baby. We end it now with another photo of Julia's children, this time with a classy, elderly lady named Woostah (Vo'estaa'e, White Cow), the graceful woman on the cover of this book. She is giving the Tuell girls their first lessons with toy bows and arrows. Julia Mae, at two, sits on her lap, too young to be very attentive. "Pinkie" (Wenonah) seems ready to try what she has learned.

The photo is entitled "First Lesson," but I would like to take it for our last, taught by Woostah, the daughter of Dull Knife, for it involves far more than children playing with bows and arrows. This woman was also once a little girl, and in the best of times she too was taught by gentle elders. But in the worst of times her family struggled in the snow with the great Dull Knife (Morning Star) as he tried to elude the soldiers chasing him down. The soldiers were enforcing a terrible order, an order to send the Northern Cheyennes south for a second time to a land they considered alien, unhealthy, a land hundreds of miles from their home and sacred ground. The Cheyennes had said they would die rather than be sent away, and many of them did, along with some of the soldiers. Woostah's brother and two sisters died.

She survived. There are those who would say that she had a right to hate. Some would even extend her the right to hate these innocent tow-headed children, because they were of the same race as those who shattered her people's way of life. But we can see no hate in Woostah. That is her lesson.

Julia Tuell said this about her: "She was a lovable woman, an aristocrat in bearing and manner, honest—the true type of a lady of noble birth. I knew her well, and she loved and fondled my children." Enough said.

Notes

Chapter 1

1. A note on Woostah (Vo'estaa'e), "White Cow" or White Buffalo Cow Woman": The stately Cheyenne woman who graces the cover of this book and appears frequently in it was made known to Julia Tuell, her good friend, in the oral Cheyenne tradition of the early century, as the daughter of Morning Star (Dull Knife). Current records do not list her among Morning Star's children, although half a dozen women with her name appear on early reservation rolls. Unfortunately, the first Cheyenne census did not list women at all, and the second only wives, not children. All this is further complicated by the fact that Plains Indians used names for family relationships in a far more expansive way than white cultures do, so "daughter" could include nieces as well as adopted children. Counsel with Paul Dyke, the artist and scholar of the northern tribes, yielded the following interpretation: No one knew Woostah better than Julia Tuell, he reminded me, and no source of information is more valid than the oral tradition that identified Woostah as Morning Star's daughter. I have abided by this wisdom.
2. Father Peter J. Powell, *Sweet Medicine* (Norman: University of Oklahoma Press, 1969), pp. 19–21.
3. *Sweet Medicine,* p. 197.
4. Varble Tuell to Dan Aadland, October 1995.
5. John Stands In Timber, *Cheyenne Memories* (Lincoln: University of Nebraska Press, 1967), p. 100.

Chapter 2

1. Frank Linderman, *Pretty-Shield: Medicine Woman of the Crows* (New York: The John Day Company, 1932), p. 9.
2. Father Peter J. Powell, *Sweet Medicine* (Norman: University of Oklahoma Press, 1969), pp. 4–5.

3. George Bird Grinnell, *The Cheyenne Indians: Their History and Ways of Life,* Vol. I (Lincoln: University of Nebraska Press, 1972), p. 145.
4. *The Cheyenne Indians,* Vol. I, pp. 131–132.
5. *Pretty-Shield,* pp. 145–147.
6. *Pretty-Shield,* pp. 148–149.
7. *Pretty-Shield,* p. 149.
8. *The Cheyenne Indians,* Vol. I, p. 161.
9. *The Cheyenne Indians,* Vol. I, pp. 160–164.

Chapter 3

1. George Bird Grinnell, *The Cheyenne Indians: Their History and Ways of Life,* Vol. I (Lincoln: University of Nebraska Press, 1972), pp. 48–50.
2. *The Cheyenne Indians,* Vol. I, pp. 48–50.
3. Mark Brown, *The Plainsmen of Yellowstone* (Lincoln: University of Nebraska Press, 1961), p. 43.
4. Frank Linderman, *Pretty-Shield: Medicine Woman of the Crows* (New York: The John Day Company, 1932), p. 95.
5. *Pretty-Shield,* pp. 93–97.
6. *The Cheyenne Indians,* Vol. I, pp. 256–257.
7. Francis Parkman, *The Oregon Trail* (New York: New American Library, 1978), pp. 175–176.
8. *The Cheyenne Indians,* Vol. I, p. 320.

Chapter 4

1. George Bird Grinnell, *The Cheyenne Indians: Their History and Ways of Life,* Vol. II (Lincoln: University of Nebraska Press, 1972), p. 160.
2. Father Peter J. Powell, *Sweet Medicine* (Norman: University of Oklahoma Press, 1969), p. 441.
3. Luther S. Kelly, *Yellowstone Kelly: The Memoirs of Luther S. Kelly,* edited by M.M. Quaife (Lincoln: University of Nebraska Press, 1926/1973), pp. 177–178.
4. Frank Linderman, *Plenty Coups: Chief of the Crows* (Lincoln: University of Nebraska Press, 1962), p. 136.
5. Robert M. Utley, *The Last Days of the Sioux Nation* (New Haven: Yale University Press, 1963), p. 108.
6. *The Cheyenne Indians,* Vol. II, p. 26.
7. *The Cheyenne Indians,* Vol. II, p. 13.

8. *The Cheyenne Indians,* Vol. II, p. 58.

9. *The Cheyenne Indians,* Vol. II, p. 50.

Chapter 5

1. Thomas E. Mails, *Sundancing at Rosebud and Pine Ridge* (Sioux Falls, South Dakota: Augustana College, 1978), p. 61.

2. *Sundancing at Rosebud and Pine Ridge,* p. 15.

3. Father Peter J. Powell, *Sweet Medicine* (Norman: University of Oklahoma Press, 1969), pp. 338–340.

4. Karl H. Schlesier, *Wolves of Heaven* (Norman: University of Oklahoma Press, 1987), p. xiii. To understand the context, the book must be read in its entirety.

5. *Sundancing at Rosebud and Pine Ridge,* p. 15.

6. George Bird Grinnell, *The Cheyenne Indians: Their History and Ways of Life,* Vol. II (Lincoln: University of Nebraska Press, 1972), p. 79.

7. *The Cheyenne Indians,* Vol. II, p. 329.

8. *Wolves of Heaven,* p. 106.

9. *Wolves of Heaven,* pp. 93–94.

SOME INTERESTING BOOKS

THE LITERATURE PERTAINING TO THE Northern Plains Indians is quite rich, so compelling is their story. For an overview of the nineteenth century in eastern Montana and the western Dakotas I have always enjoyed Mark Brown's *The Plainsmen of the Yellowstone* (Lincoln: University of Nebraska Press, 1961). Brown's thesis will be disputed by some—it's decidedly more sympathetic to the Crows and their point of view than to their Sioux and Cheyenne enemies to the east. The Sioux/Cheyenne wars of 1876–1877 have garnered unbelievable attention and have prompted the comment that more ink than blood has been spilled in conjunction with the battle of the Little Bighorn. A couple of the more recent additions that I've enjoyed are James Welch's *Killing Custer* (New York: W.W. Norton and Company, 1994) and an anthology of articles from the excellent *Montana the Magazine of Western History* edited by Paul L. Hedren and called *The Great Sioux War 1876–77* (Helena: Montana Historical Society Press, 1991). In preparing this book I found Orlan J. Svingen's *The Northern Cheyenne Indian Reservation, 1877–1900* (Niwot: University Press of Colorado, 1993) quite helpful.

Though they come from the Absaroka (Crow) culture rather than the Sioux or Cheyenne, I have quoted from two of Frank Linderman's works, both based on interviews, *Plenty Coups: Chief of the Crows* (Lincoln: University of Nebraska Press, 1962) and *Pretty-Shield: Medicine Woman of the Crows* (New York: The John Day Company, 1932). Plenty Coups's observations of the Sioux and Cheyenne are those of an enemy but admiring chief, while Pretty-Shield frankly informs us of the feminine side of a life on the Plains. These are fine books for young and old, and as a teacher I used them from ninth grade to adult levels, always with excellent response.

I have quoted also from Francis Parkman's classic, *The Oregon Trail* (New York: New American Library, 1978). While it is true that Parkman, great historian that he became, was not always aware of the import and meaning of what he observed, he had a keen eye, and I have discovered in western fiction innumerable, thinly disguised descriptions that owe their origin to *The Oregon Trail*. *Yellowstone Kelly: The Memoirs of Luther S. Kelly,* edited by M.M. Quaife (Lincoln: University of Nebraska Press, 1926/1973) is interesting for its vignettes of key Northern Plains personalities in the decade following the Civil War. John Stands in Timber's *Cheyenne Memories* (Lincoln: University of Nebraska Press, 1967) is first-rate history in an enjoyable form.

On the spiritual side, John G. Neihardt's *Black Elk Speaks* (first published in 1932, now available from Pocket Books) is a classic. So is William Bird Grinnell's *The Cheyenne Indians,* first published in 1923 and now available from Bison Books and containing photographs by Julia E. Tuell. Grinnell, of course, was the dean of Cheyenne scholars, so the serious student will investigate his other works as well. Father Peter J. Powell's two-volume work *Sweet Medicine* (Norman: University of Oklahoma Press, 1969) is a wonderful tracing of Cheyenne spirituality and is elaborated by his *People of the Sacred Mountain.* Karl H. Schlesier's *Wolves of Heaven* centers on the Massaum, its anthropological origins as well as its practice by the Cheyenne tribe. I also found very useful Thomas E. Mails's *Sundancing at Rosebud and Pine Ridge* (Sioux Falls, South Dakota: Augustana College, 1978) and Paul Dyck's *Brulé: The Sioux People of the Rosebud* (Flagstaff, Arizona: Northland Press, 1971). *Lame Deer, Seeker of Visions* by John (Fire) Lame Deer (Pocket Books) is the biography of a twentieth-century Sioux holy man.